THIS LAND OF LIBERTY

A HISTORY OF AMERICA'S JEWS

THIS LAND OF LIBERTY

A HISTORY OF AMERICA'S JEWS

Helene Schwartz Kenvin

And ye shall hallow the fiftieth year,
and proclaim liberty throughout the land
unto all the inhabitants thereof;
it shall be a jubilee unto you.

וְקִדַּשְׁתֶּם אֵת שְׁנַת הַחֲמִשִּׁים שָׁנָה

וּקְרָאתֶם דְּרוֹר בָּאָרֶץ לְכָל־יֹשְׁבֶיהָ

יוֹבֵל הוּא תִּהְיֶה לָכֶם.

LEVITICUS 25:10

BEHRMAN HOUSE PUBLISHERS

Project Editor: Nicolas D. Mandelkern
Map Artist: Kathleen Borowick

© Copyright 1986 by Helene Schwartz Kenvin
Published by Behrman House, Inc.
235 Watchung Avenue
West Orange, New Jersey 07052
Manufactured in the United States of America

1 2 3 4 5 6 7 8 9 10

ISBN 0-87441-421-0

Library of Congress Cataloging-in-Publication Data

Kenvin, Helene Schwartz.
  This land of liberty.

  Includes index.
  Summary: A junior high school textbook covering the
history of Jews in America.
  1. Jews—United States—History—Juvenile literature.
2. United States—Ethnic relations—Juvenile literature.
[1. Jews—United States—History] I. Title.
E184.J5K34 1986   973′.04924   85-30821

For my husband
HOWARD KENVIN
So very loved, so very loving

THANK YOU

Half the fun of writing this book was the people I met along the way. Some of them shared their memories, told me stories about themselves and their ancestors, and lent me treasured family photographs. This book has been enhanced greatly by their contributions, which are acknowledged after the text in the credit list for graphics.

Other people guided me through archives, gave their opinions on scholarly matters, and offered their expertise. I am grateful to: the staffs of Butler Library at Columbia University and the Jewish Division of the New York Public Library, especially Judith Fixler of the NYPL; Nina Cardin (Jewish Women's Resource Center); Flora Rothenberg and Helen Powers (National Council of Jewish Women); Rose Klepfisz and Elsa Felgran (Joint Distribution Committee); Israel Levine, Phoebe McKay, and Laraine Specter (American Jewish Congress); Dianne Esses (Sephardic Archives); Lawrence Geller, Lenore Kahn, and Thelma Schmerler (Hadassah); Mira Wolf (Russian Education Service of the Jewish Community House of Bensonhurst); Rabbi Mitchell Orlian; Bernice Balter (Women's League for Conservative Judaism); Beatrice Bullock and Donna Gloeckner (NAACP Legal Defense Fund); Rabbi Marc Angel and Joseph Turica (Shearith Israel, New York); Mary Bohm; Anita Padovano (Ticor Title Guarantee Company); Robert E. Lazar (ILGWU Archives); Martha Bergman and Jane Mitchell (Visiting Nurse Service); Eleanor Hassan Einus (ACTWU Archives); Harvis and Irv Skopp; Ann McGinn (Oglethorpe University); Ben Berger; Jay H. Greenblatt (Alliance Colony Foundation); Wendy Schlossberg and Pearl Laufer (Jewish War Veterans); Mildred Starin (Gomez House).

I have yet to meet Fannie Zelcer (American Jewish Archives) and David Starr (American Jewish Historical Society), but we have had so much correspondence and so many long telephone conversations that we have become friends. I thank them both for locating beautiful graphics from the collections of their organizations. I also received advice and encouragement from a dear friend who epitomizes the phrase "a gentleman and a scholar," Rabbi Malcolm Stern. He is an inspiration to all of his colleagues in the fields of American Jewish history and genealogy.

I worked with two editors on this project. Arthur Kurzweil was a source of constant support, enthusiasm, and ideas while I was researching and writing the book. He shared my vision and, in that uncanny way he has, seemed to know what I was thinking before I said it. Nicolas Mandelkern worked with me during the editing and production phases of the book. He has such a keen mind that even our disagreements were fun. I hope that the finished product justifies the faith that Arthur and Nick had in me.

The best is last. I am blessed with a wonderful family. Howard, Fred, Seth, and Samson Kenvin put up with all sorts of grief from me while I was involved in this project. I hope they will agree that the book was worth it.

HELENE SCHWARTZ KENVIN

CONTENTS

I · THE COLONIAL ERA

אֵיךְ נָשִׁיר אֶת־שִׁיר־יְהֹוָה עַל אַדְמַת נֵכָר.

"How shall we sing the Lord's song in a strange land?"
Psalm 137:4

"How shall we sing the Lord's song in a strange land?" These words were written about 2500 years ago by Jews who had been driven from their land and sent to exile in Babylonia. For centuries afterwards, the Jews were without a country of their own. They were a scattered people who lived in many lands and who suffered from persecution and intolerance.

Above: Moses Raphael Levy and his wife, Grace, were prominent Jews in early eighteenth-century New York. A merchant and landowner, Levy was at one time president of Shearith Israel, the first congregation in the thirteen colonies.

This book begins with the story of the Jews in the seventeenth century. It was the dawn of an exciting age. Europeans had discovered the Americas, a new world, across the Atlantic Ocean. They were building colonies, new places for people to live, where they explored new ways of doing things and thinking about the world.

In Europe, the Jews were still oppressed by old laws and customs. There were laws which restricted their civil rights and laws which made it hard for them to earn a living. They were often forbidden to own land, to work in certain professions, to join unions, or to attend universities. In many places, they had to pay special taxes just because they were Jews. Worst of all were the anti-Jewish riots that often swept across Europe, leaving thousands of Jewish homes burned and thousands of innocent Jews murdered.

Plunder of the Ghetto, *an old print showing a pogrom in Germany in 1614. The Jews were forced to wear circular badges to distinguish them from Christians. It was to escape this kind of mistreatment that Jews came to the New World.*

Among the Jews of the Old World were the Sephardim, descendants of families that had lived for generations in Spain and Portugal. Many of these families had fled Spain in 1492, or Portugal in 1497, when the Jews were ordered to leave those countries. Others had tried to avoid persecution and exile by converting to Catholicism. Among these were people called Conversos or Marranos, who pretended to be Catholics but secretly re-

A drawing called Torture of the Pulley Inflicted. *The Inquisition tortured Marranos to make them confess to the secret practicing of Judaism.*

mained Jews. The Marranos were in great danger from the Inquisition, a church court that punished Catholics whose religious beliefs and practices were different from those of the established church. If the Inquisition found out that a Marrano was still loyal to Judaism, he could be put on trial, tortured, and killed. Thousands of Marranos were burned at the stake. Others left Spain and Portugal to preserve their lives and their Jewish faith.

A few Jews, most of them Sephardim, began to think about traveling to the New World. In America, they thought, they might be able to find the equality they had been denied in Europe. Perhaps they would be allowed to live in peace and freedom with their neighbors. Filled with hope, small groups of Jews set sail for the colonies of America.

But they found that even in America, Christians were prejudiced against the Jews. This prejudice was complicated by divisions among Christians themselves. Most of the colonies had been founded by members of a particular branch of Christianity. If the Protestants of Georgia excluded Catholics from their colony, why should they admit Jews? If the followers of the Dutch Reformed Church in New Amsterdam did not permit Lutherans to worship publicly, why should they grant that freedom to Jews?

The Jewish pioneers had to fight for permission to stay in the colonies and for equality with their fellow settlers. Their story is the opening chapter of the Jewish struggle for the freedoms enjoyed by American Jews today. It begins with the first Jews who came to these shores and the mixed welcome they received.

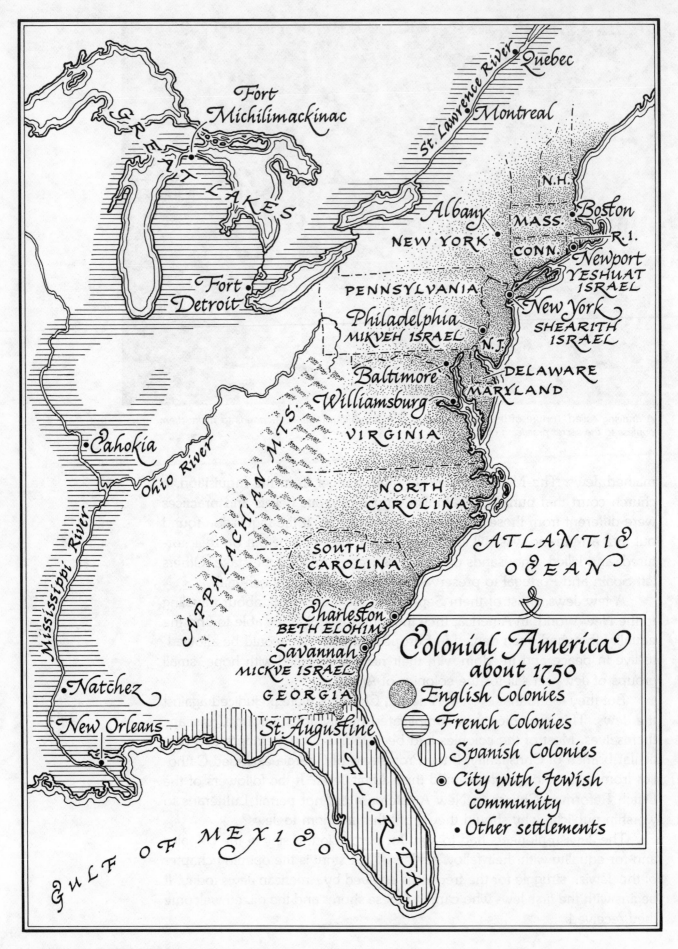

Fort Michilimackinac

Quebec

St. Lawrence River

Montreal

GREAT LAKES

N.H.

Albany

Boston

MASS.

NEW YORK

R.1.

CONN.

Newport
YESHUAT ISRAEL

Fort Detroit

PENNSYLVANIA

New York
SHEARITH ISRAEL

Philadelphia
MIKVEH ISRAEL

N.J.

Baltimore

DELAWARE

Cahokia

Ohio River

Williamsburg

MARYLAND

VIRGINIA

APPALACHIAN MTS.

NORTH CAROLINA

ATLANTIC OCEAN

Mississippi River

SOUTH CAROLINA

Charleston
BETH ELOHIM

Colonial America
about 1750

Savannah
MICKVE ISRAEL

Natchez

GEORGIA

New Orleans

St. Augustine

English Colonies

French Colonies

Spanish Colonies

FLORIDA

• City with Jewish community

• Other settlements

GULF OF MEXICO

CHAPTER ONE

THE FIRST JEWISH COMMUNITY IN AMERICA

The "Jewish Mayflower"

The first large group of Jews came to New Amsterdam. The colony had been founded by agents of the Dutch West India Company of Amsterdam, Holland, and was headed by the company's representative, Peter Stuyvesant.

The first Jewish settler in New Amsterdam was Jacob Barsimson, who arrived in August, 1654, aboard the Dutch ship *de Pereboom* ("The Peartree"). He had money to pay for his fare and a passport giving him the right to live in the colony. Stuyvesant had to let him stay.

In September, 1654, a ship called the *Sainte Catherine* anchored in the colony's harbor. It carried twenty-three Jewish refugees from the Dutch settlements in Brazil. Most of them had been living in Recife, which had a thriving Jewish community of over six hundred sugar planters, slave dealers, financiers, and merchants. When the Portuguese conquered Recife in 1654, the

A view of Recife, Brazil, printed in 1647.

Jews were afraid the Inquisition would come to Brazil and that Jews would once again be persecuted. Most of them left the colony. Twenty-three of these refugees came to New Amsterdam.

Their welcome was as cool as might be expected. They had no permits to enter the colony. In addition, they had been robbed by pirates during their trip, so they did not have money to pay for their tickets. Their goods were sold at public auction, but the amount raised wasn't enough to cover their fares. Two of them, David Israel and Moses Ambrosius, were held in jail as security until money was sent by the Jewish community in Amsterdam.

Stuyvesant Complains

Stuyvesant did not want to let Jews live in his colony. He wrote to the directors in Amsterdam that Jews were a "deceitful race" and were "repugnant" to the other settlers. "Such hateful enemies and blasphemers of the name of Christ," he said, should not "be allowed further to infect and trouble this new colony." Stuyvesant was also worried because the refugees were so poor. He was afraid that the Christians would have to support them through the coming winter. He told the directors that the Jews had been asked "in a friendly way

Isaac Aboab da Fonesca, the first rabbi in the New World, arrived in Recife in 1642. When the Portuguese conquered the city, he went back to Holland.

to depart." Where Stuyvesant expected these penniless people to go, he did not say.

To Stuyvesant's dismay, the directors replied that the Jews must be allowed to stay in New Amsterdam. They wrote that the Jews could

travel and trade to and in New Netherland and live and remain there, provided the poor among them shall not become a burden to the company or to the community, but be supported by their own nation. [S. Oppenheim, "Early History of the Jews in New York," *PAJHS*, 1909]

After Peter Stuyvesant sold all of their goods to pay for their passage, the Jews had no money and were forced to rely on the charity of the unfriendly Christian settlers.

Jewish Life in the Dutch Colony

Jews continued to arrive in New Amsterdam. Having no choice but to allow them to stay, Stuyvesant decided to make their lives so difficult that they would want to leave. Every right that was requested, every license that was applied for, was denied. The Jews asked for permission to trade in the

t' Fort nieuw Amsterdam op de Manhatans

A view of New Amsterdam published in Holland in 1655, the year after the first Jewish settlers arrived.

South (Delaware) River and Fort Orange (Albany) areas. Their requests were turned down. However, because they had already shipped goods to the South River, they were allowed to send two men there to sell them.

Salvador Dandrade made the highest bid at public auction for a house, but Stuyvesant refused to let the Jews buy real estate. Jacob Cohen Henriques' request to open a bakery was rejected. The Jews asked if they could build a synagogue and were refused permission. They petitioned for the right to serve in the citizens' militia and were excluded.

Stuyvesant Surrenders

Stuyvesant underestimated the determination of these Jewish pioneers. They drowned him with petitions and contested every rejection. In 1657, when Asser Levy's petition to be admitted as a *burgher* (a form of citizen) was denied, the Jews appealed to the

Peter Stuyvesant, governor of New Amsterdam, was known as a man with a terrible temper.

Peter Stuyvesant surrenders New Amsterdam to the British in 1664.

New Amsterdam council. They pointed out that Jews were allowed to be burghers in Amsterdam and asked, couldn't they have the same right in New Amsterdam? Ever since they had been in the colony, the Jews said, they had "borne and paid, and still bear, all Burgher burdens," such as paying taxes. Eventually, Stuyvesant had to obey the orders of the directors in Amsterdam and he allowed the Jews to become burghers.

Evening Service
OF
ROSHASHANAH,
AND
KIPPUR,
OR
The Beginning of the Year,
AND
The Day of Atonement.

NEW-YORK:
Printed by *W. Weyman*, in *Broad-Street*, MDCCLXI.

The title page of the first Rosh Hashanah-Yom Kippur prayer book published in the American colonies (1761).

Life in British New York

In 1664, ten years after the first Jews came to the Dutch colony, New Amsterdam was conquered by the British. Its name was changed to New York. The British governor was ordered to allow people of all faiths to live in the colony.

Under British rule, the life of the Jewish settlers in New York continued to improve. They could open retail shops and practice crafts. In 1730 they built the first Jewish synagogue in the colonies and called it Shearith Israel ("Remnant of Israel"). This small building on Mill Street was the first synagogue in North America.

The first synagogue in the thirteen colonies was built on Mill Street, which is now known as South William Street and is in the heart of New York's financial district. The synagogue no longer exists.

CLOSE-UPS:
Colonial New Amsterdam and New York

THE DUTCH JEWS HELP THE NEW AMSTERDAM JEWS

When Peter Stuyvesant tried to prevent Jews from settling in New Amsterdam, the Jews of Amsterdam acted quickly to help their fellow Jews in the colony. They sent a petition to the directors of the Dutch West India Company, requesting that Jews be allowed to stay in New Amsterdam.

In their petition, the Amsterdam Jews pointed out that the refugees could not go to Spain or Portugal because of the Inquisition. They reminded the directors that "in political matters," Jews in Amsterdam were "upon the same footing" as other residents in the city. Why should Jews have fewer rights in the colony? They noted that Jews were allowed to live and trade in English and French colonies. "How can your Honors forbid the same?" they asked. Finally, they argued, many Jews owned shares in the Dutch West India Company. It would be unfair to exclude Jews from a colony that was sponsored by the company.

When the directors ordered Stuyvesant to allow Jews to settle in New Amsterdam, they admitted that their decision was based in part on the fact that a "large amount of capital" was invested in the company by Jews. It was also influenced, they said, by "a certain petition" presented to them by the Jews of Amsterdam.

THE RIGHT TO SERVE IN THE MILITARY

In 1655, the New Amsterdam council discussed whether Jews who lived in the city should be allowed

The New Amsterdam council suggested that if the Jews were too poor to pay the tax, they could always leave the colony.

to participate in the citizens' militia. The council observed "the disgust and unwillingness of [the members of the militia] to be fellow soldiers with [the Jews] and to be on guard with them in the same guardhouse." It was decided that the Jews should "remain exempt from the general training and guard duty," but instead would have to pay a special tax.

Asser Levy and Jacob Barsimson protested, saying they were too poor to pay the tax because "they must earn their living by manual labor." Levy's petition must have been granted. In 1657, when he requested that he be admitted as a burgher, he said that he had kept "watch and ward like any other Burgher," that is, that he had done his military service.

FIGHTING FOR RELIGIOUS FREEDOM

Peter Stuyvesant wrote to the directors in Amsterdam that if freedom of religion was granted to the Jews, "we cannot refuse the Lutherans and Papists [Catholics]." In March 1656, the directors replied that the Jews should be granted "civil and political liberties, without the said Jews becoming thereby entitled to a license to exercise and carry on their religion in synagogues or gatherings." Stuyvesant responded that the Jews "have many times requested of us the free and public exercise of their abominable religion, but this cannot yet be accorded to them."

Dutch Jews celebrating Sukkot in the famous synagogue of Amsterdam.

Jewish services held during Stuyvesant's time must have taken place in private homes, because he never let the Jews build a synagogue. However, he did allow them to buy land outside the city for a cemetery.

A 1695 map of New York indicates "the Jewes Synagogue" on Beaver Street. This must have referred to a house that was used as a synagogue. The congregation, Shearith Israel, had about twenty families. They were led by Saul Brown, the first Jewish religious leader in New York.

It was not until 1730 that the congregation built a small synagogue on Mill Street. It was only about thirty-five square feet, but it was the first Jewish house of worship built in the colonies.

This Torah headpiece is one of a pair made for Shearith Israel by the colonial Jewish silversmith Myer Myers.

An excerpt from the 1761 minute book of Shearith Israel, written in Portuguese, showing the signatures of Jacob Franks and Uriah Hendricks, officers of the synagogue.

"The Little Synagogue," a small chapel in the building on West 70th Street that currently houses Congregation Shearith Israel, has many of the original furnishings from the Mill Street synagogue. Among them are the tebah (reader's desk), the railing, and the straight-backed benches on the south wall.

THE FRANKS FAMILY

Jacob Franks, a president of Shearith Israel, was a successful New York merchant who traded in dry goods, liquor, and slaves. His wife, Bilhah Abigail Levy Franks (daughter of Moses Levy), once wrote to her son:

> Your father is Very full of buissness. I never knew the benifit of the Sabath before but Now I am Glad when it comes for his Sake that he may have a Little relaxation from that Continuall Hurry he is in.

Abigail led a group of women who helped to raise money to build Shearith Israel's first synagogue. Her committee included: Simha de Torres, Rachel Luis, Judith Pacheco, Hannah Michaels, and Miriam Lopez de Fonseca. One could say these women were members of the first synagogue sisterhood in America.

The Franks were deeply distressed when their daughter Phila eloped with Oliver Delancey, son of a prominent Christian family. They did not speak to her for over a year. Abigail wrote:

> My spirits was for some time soe depresst that it was a pain for me to speak or see anyone. I have overcome it soe far as not to make my concern soe conspicuous but I shall never have that serenity nor peace within I have soe happyly had hittherto. My house has bin my prison ever since. [AJHS, *Letters of the Franks Family*]

By the end of the eighteenth century, the descendants of the Franks family had intermarried, assimilated, and disappeared as Jews.

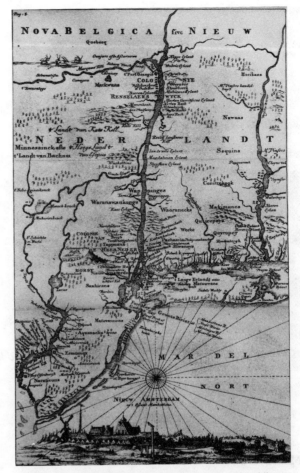

An old map of the Hudson Valley, showing the Albany-Esopus area where Lucena traded.

Abigail and Jacob Franks

A HUDSON RIVER TRADER

Jacob Lucena arrived in New Amsterdam in 1656. He became a trader and in 1678 he asked for a permit to trade in Albany and Esopus, in the Hudson River valley. In his petition, he wrote that he

> hath been a dweller in this collony by the space of twenty-two yeares and upwards, hath served an apprenticeship and been a trader for himselfe by the space of eight yeares and upwards, and hath kept house, fire and candle, watching and training. . . . [Jacob R. Marcus, *Early American Jewry*]

Lucena said that although in the past he had been allowed to trade freely in the Albany-Esopus area, he was now being prevented from doing so for lack of a license. Perhaps this was because he was not a citizen and had no right to trade; or because he was a Jew; or because the other traders wanted to prevent competition from him. Lucena finally did get his pass and was able to ship his goods up the Hudson.

Asser Levy was also active in this region. He owned land in Albany (registered to him as "Asser Levy Van Swellam") and may have had trading privileges there as well.

Left: Gomez House from the outside. The second story was added by another owner during the revolutionary war. Right: One of the two huge fireplaces in the living room at Gomez House.

GOMEZ HOUSE

Luis Moses Gomez was a refugee from the Spanish Inquisition who came to New York about 1703. Some time between 1714 and 1720, Gomez and his sons built a single-story stone house near what is now Newburgh, New York. The property was at the junction of several Indian trails, and the house was used as a trading post. Gomez House may be the oldest house still standing in America that was built by a Jew.

Because the house was in an isolated area, it has thick walls and looks like a fortress. It also has a hidden passageway that leads underground to the stream known as "Jews' Creek." Was this an emergency escape route to be used if there was an Indian attack? Or was it a reminder of the days when the Gomez family were secret Jews in Catholic Spain, and always had to be ready to run from the Inquisition?

Gomez was a leader of Shearith Israel. He and his son Daniel wrote to the Jews in Jamaica for financial assistance in the construction of the Mill Street synagogue. At his death, Gomez left to his son Mordecai, "one pare of Silver Adornements for the five Books of Moses weying Thirty nine ounces. . . ."

The secret door behind this bookcase leads to an underground escape tunnel.

FROM OUR JEWISH HERITAGE: Charity

Peter Stuyvesant was afraid that the Jewish refugees who came to New Amsterdam would become a burden on the community because they were so poor. But he had no cause to worry, since Jews in Amsterdam sent money to support the Jews in the colony. Jews have always taken care of each other. What does our Jewish heritage teach us about our obligation to help the needy?

Sharing God's World

The word that is used in Hebrew to describe acts of charity is *tzedakah*. It does not actually mean "charity," but "righteousness" or "justice." Why do the rabbis use this word when they talk about helping those in need?

The Jewish laws about tzedakah are based upon the understanding that everything in the world belongs to God. If some people possess a larger part of God's world, it is only proper that they share what they have with those who have less. So when the rabbis speak of charity, they are really talking about doing what is right or just.

Tzedakah in the Bible: The Torah commands that grapes or grain dropped by harvesters must be left for the poor. (Leviticus 19:9–10; Deuteronomy 29:19) Here, Ruth gathers grain in the field of Boaz. (Ruth 2:3)

The Importance of Tzedakah

The Torah teaches that God "executes justice for the fatherless and the widow, and loves the stranger, giving him food and clothing." (Deuteronomy 10:18) Just as God is charitable, so too must God's people be charitable. Abraham and his descendants were singled out so that they could "keep the way of the Lord, to do righteousness [tzedakah] and justice." (Genesis 18:19)

The Talmud says that the world is based on three things: the Torah, prayer, and charity. One rabbi believed that the giving of charity is equal to all of the other commandments put together. Throughout our sacred writings those who are charitable are praised. The woman of valor "opens her hand to the poor, and reaches out her hands to the needy." (Proverbs 31:20) The man "who is kind to the poor" will be repaid by the Lord. (Proverbs 19:17)

Giving charity is a way of expressing faith in God. According to the prophet Ezekiel, one of the reasons why the city of Sodom was destroyed was that its people "did not aid the poor and needy." (Ezekiel 16:49)

The seal of the Hebrew Benevolent Society, founded in Charleston, South Carolina in 1784. It was one of the first charitable organizations in the United States.

How to be Charitable

There are many forms of tzedakah. Maimonides, a Jewish scholar, listed eight ways of being charitable, each level considered better than the one before it. He said that the lowest form of tzedakah is to give money reluctantly and in small amounts. The highest form is to help someone to help himself. Examples of the best kind of charity are giving a needy person a job or helping to pay for someone's education.

Giving money is an important part of tzedakah. But not all acts of charity involve money. Doing something kind for someone in need is equally important. As the Talmud teaches, "Deeds of love are performed with one's money and with one's person." Visiting the sick, taking care of those who are old, collecting food and clothing for the poor, are all forms of charity. Tzedakah is knowing how to give of yourself when you are needed.

The Jews' Hospital in New York, founded in 1852. It is now housed in a huge, modern complex and called Mount Sinai Hospital.

Nurses and children in the Hebrew Sheltering Guardian Society orphanage in New York (1903), founded to care for neglected and abandoned children.

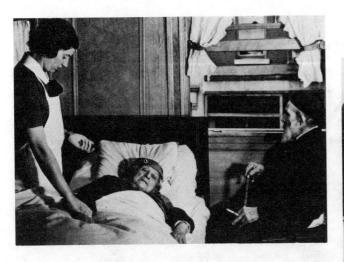

Tzedakah in America: (starting from top left) A visiting nurse with a sick old woman. Bottom left: Hadassah volunteers packing toys and books collected by students for children who survived the Holocaust. Top right: Eleanor Roosevelt (left), wife of the president, in a Congress House during World War Two. These houses were run by the Women's Division of the American Jewish Congress as community centers for people in the armed forces. Middle right: A United Jewish Appeal breakfast to raise money for Israel. Bottom right: The Friends of Refugees of Eastern Europe (FREE) distributing Pesah food to recent immigrants from the Soviet Union (1985).

CHAPTER TWO
JEWS IN COLONIAL NEW ENGLAND

Massachusetts Bay Colony

The Puritans who controlled the Massachusetts Bay Colony were fascinated by the ancient Hebrews. They studied the Hebrew language and Bible. They gave biblical names to their children and their towns. Unfortunately, the Puritan love of the ancient Hebrew did not extend to their modern descendants—the Jews.

Although few Jews lived in Massachusetts Bay during the seventeenth and eighteenth centuries, some did pass through. In 1649, the records of the colony note a gift to "Solomon Franco ye Jew." Unable to collect money due him from a business associate, Franco had been stranded in Boston without funds. He was paid six shillings a week from the colonial treasury until he could arrange for passage back to Holland. Some scholars say that the Puritans paid for his upkeep because they were so glad to get rid of him. It is also reported that a Jew named Solomon was prosecuted in 1668 for traveling through a Massachusetts town on Sunday, the Christian sabbath, when all travel was forbidden.

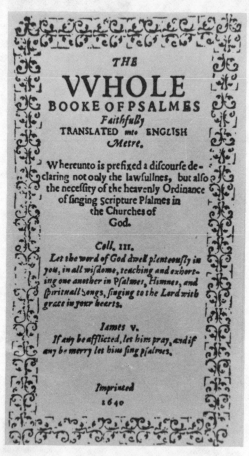

The first book published in the English colonies was the Bay Psalm Prayer Book (1640), a translation of Tehillim, the biblical Book of Psalms.

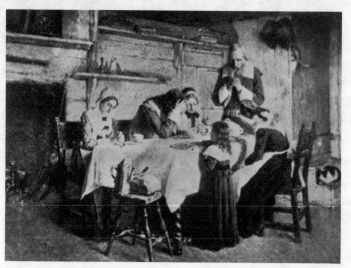

Invoking God's Blessing, by the Jewish artist Henry Mosler, pictures New England colonists at prayer.

Boston

The 1674 tax list for Boston names Rowland Gideon "ye Jew," who paid at a rate of 18 shillings. In 1675 Gideon sued to recover money due him on a business matter involving tobacco.

Michael Asher and Isaac Solomon were merchants who came to Boston from New York. Between the years 1710 and 1720, they had a partnership and traded in tobacco and snuff. Solomon once wrote to Mordecai Gomez in New York that he would "take it as a great feavour" (favor) if, instead of sending him some money he was owed, Gomez would "send me for my money, if it is to be bought there, a Yom Kippur *tefilah* [prayer book]." The first Jewish congregation in Boston, Ohabei Shalom, was not established until 1842.

Newport

When Roger Williams was banished from Massachusetts because his opinions differed from those of the established church, he founded a settlement in Rhode Island. Jewish merchants and shipowners were attracted to the Rhode Island city of Newport, which had a natural harbor and a growing international trade. Jews from the West Indies, Europe, and New York came to the city. By 1677, Moses Pachecho and Mordecai Campanell were allowed to buy land for a cemetery.

Trade and Naturalization

Although Jews were allowed freedom of religion in Rhode Island, they were not permitted to become naturalized. This concerned them, because according to the British Navigation Act of 1660, only naturalized citizens could engage in trade. The purpose of these laws was to prevent involvement "by Jews, French, and other foreigners" in the profitable colonial trade.

The colonial authorities often ignored the law, but sometimes they did enforce it. In 1685, William Dyre, an official of Rhode Island, brought an action against a group of Jewish residents of Newport including Mor-

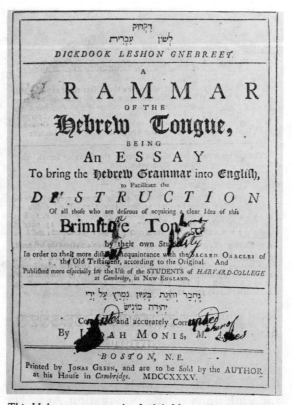

This Hebrew grammar by Judah Monis, the first Hebrew book printed in North America, was published in Boston in 1735. Born a Jew, Monis converted to Christianity and then was appointed an instructor of Hebrew at Harvard College. A student doodler has changed this grammar for the "instruction" of students "by their own study" to one for their "destruction . . . by their own stupidity."

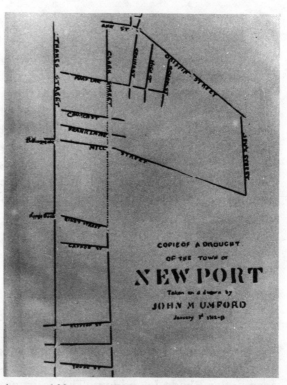

A map of Newport, 1712–13, showing "Jew's Street" on the right.

A copy of the court record in the 1685 suit by Dyre against the Jews of Newport.

decai and Abraham Campanell, Saul Brown, Abraham Burgis, Rachel Mendez, "and other Jews foreigne borne." The court records are not complete, but they indicate that the Jews were charged as "aliens," perhaps for violations of the Navigation Act. The case was dropped when Dyre failed to appear in court. However, the continuing threat to their livelihood was one of the reasons why Jews throughout the colonies were eager to be naturalized.

The Naturalization Act of 1740

The situation began to change in 1740, when the British Parliament passed the Naturalization Act. This allowed foreign-born Jews who were living in the colonies to become naturalized. They did not get full political rights, but they were now allowed to participate in trade. The act was designed to encourage emigration to the colonies. A large population was thought to be a "means of advancing the wealth and strength of any nation or country."

An eighteenth-century scene showing colonial merchants on a dock.

Jews Petition for Naturalization

In 1761, Newport residents Aaron Lopez and Isaac Elizer applied to be naturalized. Their petition was denied on the grounds that only Christians could become naturalized under Rhode Island law. The court got around the 1740 Naturalization Act by say-

A page from the shipping book of Aaron Lopez. Among the items shipped is tongue which, according to the Hebrew word on the left, is kosher.

ing that it was intended only to encourage population growth. As Rhode Island was now crowded enough, the court decided, the act didn't apply. Lopez moved to Massachusetts and was naturalized there, while Elizer got his papers in New York.

Impact of the Court's Action

When the Lopez-Elizer petitions to the Rhode Island court were denied, Ezra Stiles, a Christian minister who had many friends in the Newport Jewish community, was present in court. He wrote in his diary:

> I remark that Providence seems to make every Thing to work for Mortification to the Jews, & to prevent their incorporating into any Nation; that thus they may continue a distinct people. [Franklin Dexter, editor, *Itineraries of Ezra Stiles*]

Stiles felt that it was the will of God that the Jews had not been made citizens, so that they would not assimilate and disappear. He thought that "the Jews will never become incorporated with the people of America, any more than in Europe, Asia, and Africa."

In spite of the restrictions on their civil rights, the Jews of Newport continued to prosper. In 1763 the community completed its first synagogue.

Oath of naturalization of Aaron Lopez in Massachusetts. The words, "upon the true faith of a Christian" have been crossed out.

CLOSE-UPS: *Colonial Newport*

AMERICA'S OLDEST SYNAGOGUE

In 1759, members of the Newport Jewish community sent a letter to their fellow Jews at Shearith Israel in New York, asking for money to help build a synagogue. During the Passover festival, the New Yorkers collected almost one hundred fifty pounds "towards building at Newport a place of worship to Almighty God." The leaders of Shearith Israel wrote: "We sincerely wish you success in all your laudable undertakings, and that our God may graciously enable his people to do *mitsvoth* [commandments]."

Because of high building costs and difficulties in raising money, the synagogue was not completed until 1763. The ḥazan ("reader," a Sephardic name for the man who leads prayer services) was a Dutch Jew named Isaac Touro. His sons, Abraham and Judah, gave funds for the care of the synagogue, which later became known as the Touro Synagogue. Although it was not the first synagogue built in this country, Touro is the oldest synagogue still standing.

This trapdoor under the reader's desk leads to an escape tunnel. Perhaps the synagogue's founders put it there because of their memories of the Inquisition. Many of them came from Spain and Portugal, where Judaism was illegal. They were used to observing their religion in secret, hiding whenever authorities approached.

Left: Yeshuat Yisrael ("Salvation of Israel"), now known as Touro synagogue. Right: One of a pair of Torah headpeices made for the Newport congregation by the colonial silversmith Myer Myers.

The interior of the synagogue in Newport.

Rabbi Ḥaim Isaac Karigal

A TRAVELER FROM THE HOLY LAND

A highlight of the year 1773 for Newport's Jewish community was the five-month visit by Rabbi Ḥaim Isaac Karigal from Hebron in the land of Israel. Born in 1733, the rabbi had been ordained at the age of seventeen and had spent much of his life traveling throughout the world raising funds for Jews in the Holy Land.

During his stay in Newport, Karigal became friendly with Ezra Stiles, the Protestant minister. Stiles described Karigal as "a large Man, neat and well dressed in the Turkish habit." At their first meeting, Stiles and Karigal "conversed largely on the Gemara, the 2 Talmuds (of which he preferred the Babylonish), the Changes of the Hebrew Language in different ages."

Along with other invited officials from the colony, Stiles attended services at the Newport synagogue on *Shevuot*. Karigal delivered a forty-seven minute sermon in Spanish and Hebrew on "The Salvation of Israel." Karigal's "Oratory, Elocution and Gestures were fine and oriental," Stiles wrote. "It was very animated."

Some say this candle holder in the Newport synagogue was brought from Spain by the Sephardim who founded the congregation.

The printed text of Rabbi Karigal's Shevuot sermon.

JACOB RODRIGUEZ RIVERA

Jacob Rodriguez Rivera was born in Spain and came to Newport in 1748. He had been naturalized in New York, so he was able to participate in Newport's thriving trade. Rivera was a successful businessman and merchant shipper, best known for his role in the spermaceti industry. (Spermaceti, a wax that comes from whales, was used to make candles.) Together with a group of business colleagues, Rivera formed an association to regulate competition. Most of his partners were Christians, but out of respect for Rivera they held no meetings on the Jewish Sabbath.

Rivera was a founder and president of Yeshuat Yisrael, the Newport congregation. Rivera and his son-in-law Aaron Lopez donated over ten thousand feet of lumber for the construction of a building at Rhode Island College, later known as Brown University.

Jacob Rodriguez Rivera

Aaron Lopez

Sarah Lopez and her son Joshua

THE LOPEZ FAMILY

Duarte and Anna Lopez were Marranos from Portugal whom, as Lopez put it, God "delivered from the reach of Barbarous Inquisition." When they moved to Newport in 1752 they returned to Judaism. Duarte was circumcised and changed his name to Aaron. Anna changed her name to Abigail and they were remarried in a Jewish ceremony. Abigail died in 1762, and a year later Aaron married Sarah Rivera, daughter of Jacob Rodriguez Rivera.

In 1767, Lopez wrote to Abraham I. Abrahams, teacher and circumciser for Shearith Israel in New York:

> I have the singular pleasure of addressing you on the joyfull Occasion that presents me the arrival of a Brother of mine from Portugal with his Wife & three sons; Their Errand being founded on the Grand Object of Glorifying the protector of Israel, are inspired with a Spark of Our Old Father's Zeal & ready to obey the Divine precept.
> Therefore earnestly entreat your Devotion to Lead you to be the meretorious Instrument of their Obtaining the Covenant which happily Characterize us a peculiar Flock. [Newport Historical Society]

Abrahams came to Newport for the circumcisions and later sent Lopez several sets of *tzitzits* (ritual fringed garments) for his family.

A rich and successful merchant, Lopez was a leader of Yeshuat Yisrael Congregation in Newport and was well-known for his charity. He remained an observant Jew and did not send his ships out or conduct business on the Sabbath or Jewish holidays.

CHAPTER THREE

JEWS IN THE SOUTHERN COLONIES

Savannah

In the early 1700s, London was filled with Jewish refugees. They came from Germany, Poland, and the countries of the Inquisition, and soon became a burden on the established Jewish community. The leaders of the London synagogue, Bevis Marks, decided to send some of the refugees to Georgia, a new colony established in 1732 by a group of English Protestants. Georgia's trustees tried to stop them, declaring that "no Jews should be sent," but they were too late. Jewish leaders had already chartered the ship that would carry the first Jewish settlers to Savannah.

The interior of Bevis Marks Synagogue in London, whose congregation sponsored the first Jewish settlers in Savannah.

Oglethorpe's "Welcome"

The ship arrived in July 1733. Savannah's leader, James Oglethorpe, asked a lawyer in Charleston whether he had to let the Jews stay. He was told that since the colony's charter allowed liberty of worship to all but Catholics, the Jews could not be excluded. Oglethorpe was also influenced by the fact that among the Jewish pioneers was a doctor, Samuel Nunes, who helped stop the epidemic that was sweeping through Savannah and had already claimed twenty lives.

The Trustees Respond

Meanwhile, Oglethorpe received a letter from London:

James Oglethorpe

> The Trustees have heard with concern of the arrival of Forty Jews with a design to settle in Georgia. They hope they will

A view of Savannah sent to the trustees in London in 1734, not long after the arrival of the first Jews in the colony. The plots of land received by prominent Jewish settlers are numbered: (1) Benjamin Sheftall; (2) Dr. Samuel Nunes; (3) Abraham Minis; (4) Abraham De Lyon; (5) Isaac Nunes Henriques.

meet with no sort of encouragement, and desire, Sir, you will use your best endeavours that the said Jews may be allowed no kind of settlement with any of the grantees, the Trustees being apprehensive they will be of prejudice to the Trade and Welfare of the Colony. ["A Brief Account of the Establishment of the Colony of Georgia," in Peter Force, editor, *Tracts and Other Papers*, I, no. 2]

A month later, when the trustees heard about the work of Dr. Nunes, they wrote that they were "much pleased with the Behaviour of the Jewish Physician and the Service he has been to the Sick." They suggested that Oglethorpe reward him in some way, so long as the Jews were not given any land. The trustees had decided that the Jews should be removed from the colony of Georgia. But Oglethorpe had already given large grants of land to every Jewish family.

Living in Savannah

The experience of Jews in Savannah was the opposite of that in New Amsterdam. Stuyvesant had tried to restrict their rights, only to be told by the directors in Europe that they should be treated more fairly. In Georgia, it was the trustees in Europe who tried to limit Jewish settlement. Once Oglethorpe decided to admit them, the Jews were able to "enjoy all privileges the same as other colonists," a Protestant minister wrote at the time. They were even allowed to carry "muskets like the others in military style."

The Colony Flounders

Within nine years of the founding of Savannah, large numbers of the original Jewish colonists had left. The economy had been failing because of restrictions placed on the settlers by the trustees, including their refusal to allow the use of slaves.

In addition, the English were at war with the Spanish in Florida and there were fears that the Spanish might capture Savannah. This was especially worrisome to the Jews, most of whom were Sephardim. They were afraid that if the Spanish came to Savannah, the Inquisition would not be far behind. Because of this, many of the Jews left Savannah. When the threat of Spanish invasion ended and the restrictions on the colony's economic life were lifted, Jews began to drift back to Savannah.

Charleston

Jews were attracted to Charleston both because of its beautiful port and because of the relatively liberal attitude towards them in the Carolinas. An act passed in 1697 granted all foreigners living in the Carolinas the same rights as anyone born of English parents, if they applied for naturalization. Among the first who did so were the Jewish merchants Simon Valentine (nephew of New York's Asser Levy), Jacob Mendis, and Abraham Avila. A few years later, Valentine became the first Jew to own land in the Carolinas.

Political Rights

The Carolina election law of 1721 allowed "every free white man . . . professing the Christian religion" the right to vote, if he was over twenty-one and owned property. Those who held public office had to be sworn on the Christian Bible. Yet the Jews of South Carolina were known to have voted, and in 1774, an English Jew named Francis Salvador was elected to the South Carolina Provincial Congress. It would seem that South Carolina had strict laws, but that they were often ignored.

Jewish Life

The Charleston Jewish community became firmly established in the 1740s. In 1749 a congregation was formed called Beth Elohim (House of God). Isaac da Costa was the *ḥazan*. The *ḥaham* ("wise man," a Se-

The port of Charleston, South Carolina, about 1750.

phardic title for rabbi) was Moses Cohen, who supported himself as a shopkeeper. The congregation did not build a synagogue until 1794, but its cemetery on Coming Street, founded in 1762, is one of the oldest in the South.

The Coming Street Cemetery of the Beth Elohim synagogue, Charleston.

The interior and exterior of the Beth Elohim synagogue, Charleston, as drawn by the Jewish artist Solomon Nunes Carvalho. The synagogue burned down in the great fire that swept the city in 1838.

CLOSE-UPS: *Southern Colonial Jews*

COLONIAL SHEFTALLS

Benjamin and Perla Sheftall were on the first ship that brought Jews to Savannah. Their son Mordecai was born in Georgia in 1735. Thirteen years later, Benjamin sent to England, requesting bar mitzvah instruction books for his son. When the books were delayed, Benjamin wrote to a friend:

> I live [leave] Your Honour to guess in what grife [grief] I am in to be misfortenable, my eldest son b[e]ing three months ago thirteen years of age, and I not to have any frauntlets [*tefilin*] nor books fit for him. [David T. Morgan, "Judaism in Eighteenth Century Georgia," *Georgia Historical Quarterly*.]

A successful merchant and distinguished patriot during the revolutionary war, Mordecai married Frances Hart, daughter of a family from The Hague. The Sheftalls were religious Jews who ate only kosher food. Once when going to visit a non-Jewish friend who lived far from the city, Sheftall took along a sharp knife so that he could slaughter a sheep according to Jewish law to eat while there. In 1773, Sheftall donated five acres of land to the Jewish community of Savannah for use as a cemetery.

Mordecai Sheftall

Frances Hart Sheftall

THE MINIS FAMILY

Among the first Jewish settlers in Georgia were Abraham and Abigail Minis, their daughters Leah and Esther, and Abraham's brother, Simon. In 1735, Abigail gave birth to a son, Philip, the first European boy born in Georgia.

Both Minis brothers were given plots of land by Oglethorpe. But according to a 1738 report, Abraham's land was in a swamp "so frequently under water" that he was unable to drain and farm it. He became a trader and was known to have done business with Jacob Franks of New York. Minis was described by a Christian of the times as "a Jew Freeholder here . . . who was looked upon by all of us as an honest man."

In 1741, when most of Savannah's Jews fled the city, only the Minis and Sheftall families remained. They were of German origin and had less reason to fear a Spanish invasion.

> Abraham & Abigail Minis
> arrived in Savannah, 1733
>
> Philip Minis (1734-1789) married Judith Polock
>
> Isaac Minis (1780-1856) married Divina Cohen
>
> Abram Minis (1820-1889) married Lavinia Florance
>
> Abram Minis (1859-1939) married Mabel A. Henry
>
> Abram Minis, Jr. of Savannah, Georgia (1903-   )

More than 250 years after Abraham and Abigail Minis came to Savannah, the city is still home to some of their descendants.

Torah scrolls brought to Savannah in 1733 and 1737. Right: One of the scrolls shown open.

JUDAISM IN SAVANNAH

According to the diary of Benjamin Sheftall, the first shipload of Jews to Savannah

> brought with them a Safertora [*Sefer Torah*] with two Cloaks and a Circumcision box which was given to them by Mr. Lindo a merchant in London for the use of the Congregation that they intended to establish. [Malcolm Stern, "The Sheftall Diaries," *AJHQ*]

A second Torah scroll, a *ḥanukiah* (Ḥanukah lamp), and books were later shipped from London. Sheftall noted that the Jews met together and "agreed to open a synagogue" named Mickve Israel. He did not mean that they built one. In 1738, a Protestant minister named John Bolzius reported that the Jews were holding services "in an old and miserable hut."

The Minis and Sheftall families were Ashkenazim. The rest of the Jewish colonists were Sephardim.

Bolzius wrote that this distinction caused problems within the Jewish community:

> Some Jews in Savannah complained to me the other day that the Spanish and Portuguese Jews persecute the German Jews in a way no Christian would persecute another Christian. . . . The Spanish and Portuguese Jews are not so strict insofar as eating is concerned as the others are. They eat, for instance, the beef that comes from the warehouse or that is sold anywhere else. The German Jews . . . would rather starve than eat [non-kosher] meat they do not slaughter themselves. . . . They do not know if they will ever get permission from the Trustees to build a synagogue. It will be quite some time. . . . [T]he Spanish and Portuguese Jews are against the German Jews and they are going to protest the petition by the German Jews to build a synagogue. [Malcolm Stern, "New Light on the Jewish Settlement in Savannah," *The American Jewish Experience*]

Isaac De Lyon

A CHARLESTON MERCHANT AND ḤAZAN

Isaac Da Costa had studied Jewish sacred subjects in London prior to coming to the New World. In addition to his responsibilities as *ḥazan* of the Charleston congregation, Da Costa was also treasurer of the local Masonic lodge.

In 1755, Da Costa formed a partnership with Thomas Farr, Jr., to trade corn, flour, rum, cider, and slaves. They dealt in both European and Indian goods.

Newspaper announcement of Lindo's appointment as Surveyor General and Inspector of Indigo.

MOSES LINDO OF CHARLESTON

Moses Lindo first arrived in Charleston in 1756 to buy indigo, a dye used in the English textile industry. In 1762, forty-eight Christians petitioned the governor that he be appointed Surveyor and Inspector General of Indigo for the Carolinas. Lindo was largely responsible for the establishment of the indigo industry in South Carolina. It became the second most important crop after rice, and brought great wealth to the colony.

Lindo gave money to Rhode Island College (now Brown University) because it allowed Jews to attend.

THE DE LYON FAMILY

Abraham De Lyon was listed among the passengers on the first boatload of Jews that came to Savannah. His wife, Esther, daughter of Dr. Nunes, arrived some months later with their daughters Rebecca and Rachel.

De Lyon grew up in Portugal, where he had experience growing grapes and making wine. There were high hopes that he would be able to introduce this industry to Georgia. He was given land by Oglethorpe and a special loan to promote his work. It was reported that he had grown "several kinds of grapes in his garden, and, amongst others, the Porto and Malaga to great perfection."

In 1741, his fear of Spaniards led him to flee north with the rest of the Sephardic Jews in the Savannah community. One of the trustees pointed out that that although De Lyon's own effort failed because he abandoned his vineyard, "others, who by his example took to planting vines," had great success.

De Lyon's son Isaac was born in Savannah in 1739. He was taken to Charleston with the family, but returned to Savannah in 1762.

Processing indigo in South Carolina.

CHAPTER FOUR

JEWS IN THE OTHER COLONIES

Early Pennsylvania Traders

The first Jews in Pennsylvania went there to trade with the Indians. In 1655, when Peter Stuyvesant refused to give the Dutch Jews a permit to trade at the Delaware River on Pennsylvania's eastern border, he allowed them to send Isaac Israel and Isaac Cardozo to sell the goods they had already purchased.

A year later the New Amsterdam Jews received permission to trade in the area and some may have settled there. An Indian treaty made at Fort Casimir in 1657 was signed by Isaac Masa, identified as "a Jew." Another Indian trader, Isaac Miranda from Tuscany, lived at Conoy Creek in Lancaster County in 1715. He converted to Christianity, but continued to be known as the "apostate Jew or fashionable Christian."

Philadelphia

The charter of William Penn's colony allowed freedom of worship. But in order to be a freeman in Pennsylvania—to vote or hold office—men had to own property and "possess faith in Jesus Christ." After the 1740 Naturalization Act was passed, Jews could be naturalized in Pennsylvania but still could not vote or hold office.

In the mid-eighteenth century, Jewish merchants were attracted to Philadelphia, the last of the five colonial port cities to have a substantial Jewish community. Among the most prominent of these were Nathan Levy and David Franks, sons of New York businessmen Moses Levy and Jacob Franks. The younger Levy and Franks were models of the extremes of Jewish religious life in their time. Levy was

Some of the Jews who traded with Indians managed to keep kosher even in the wilderness. They ate only hard-boiled eggs and other food they brought with them, fruit and wild berries from the forest, and fish they caught in local streams.

Colonial Philadelphia, as seen from the New Jersey bank of the Delaware River.

devoted to Shearith Israel in New York and sent large amounts of money for its support. He was one of the first practicing Jews in Philadelphia and obtained land for the first Jewish cemetery there. Franks also contributed to Shearith Israel and observed *shloshim* (the thirty-day mourning period) when his father died. But he married a Christian and raised his children in a Christian home.

Ties Among Colonial Jews

Barnard and Michael Gratz were also among the successful Jewish merchants in prerevolutionary Philadelphia. Their relationship with Joseph Simon of Lancaster, Pennsylvania was typical of that of many Jews in colonial America. The three men shared a devotion to their Jewish heritage and all were founders and financial supporters of Mikveh Israel, the first congregation in Philadelphia. They were also united by family ties: Simon and Barnard Gratz married women who were first cousins, while Michael Gratz was married to Simon's daughter, Miriam. In addition, they had many business dealings together. Such common bonds of religion, kinship, and joint commercial enterprise united the Jewish communities across colonial boundaries.

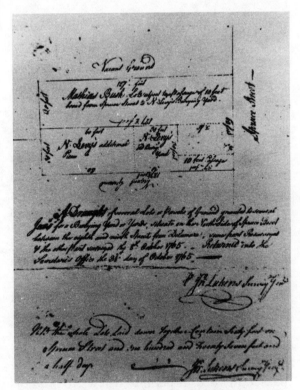

The plan of the Spruce Street Cemetery, showing the land acquired by Nathan Levy.

Catholic Maryland

Maryland was founded by Catholics. In 1649, the Law Concerning Religion made it a crime punishable by death to deny that Jesus was the son of God. In 1656 a man named Jacob Lumbrozo, known as the "Jew doctor," arrived in Maryland from Portugal. Lumbrozo was arrested in 1658 because witnesses claimed that he had said Jesus was a man, not God, whose "miracles" were performed by magic. Lumbrozo's defense, according to court records, was that he had been forced to enter into a debate on religion.

> Being by profession a Jew he answered to some particular demands then urged, & as to that of miracles done by Art magick, he declared what remains concerning Moses & the Magicians of Egipt; but sayd not anything scoffingly or in derogation by him Christians acknowledge for their Messias [Messiah]. [*Maryland Archives* XLI]

Lumbrozo was jailed for a time, but was freed during a general pardon.

The Maryland Law Concerning Religion.

Justice for Jews

Maryland court records mention a successful lawsuit in 1755 by Sampson Levy, an early Jewish resident of Baltimore. This shows that by the eighteenth century, Jews in Maryland could obtain justice in the courts. But since they were ineligible to vote, hold office, or conduct public worship services, few Jews came to colonial Maryland. Jews did not receive full equality in Maryland until the nineteenth century. After many efforts by Solomon Etting, Jacob I. Cohen, and a Catholic legislator named Thomas Kennedy, a "Jew Bill" was finally passed in 1826. It permitted Jews to hold office in Maryland without taking a Christian oath. Solomon Etting, who had worked so hard for this law, was promptly elected to the Baltimore city council. Four years later, in Baltimore, a group of Jews established the state's first synagogue.

The Colonial Era

Estimates of the number of Jews in America at the end of the colonial era range from under one thousand to about twenty-five hundred. Most of the earliest settlers were Sephardim, but long before the Revolution, most of the Jews in America were Ashkenazim, Jews from Central and Eastern Europe. However, they continued to follow Sephardic ritual in the synagogues.

These Jewish pioneers braved rough ocean voyages and an uncertain future in the New World only to be rejected by other settlers and denied equal rights. But they struggled hard for equality and eventually they won, partly because the other colonists realized that the Jews were making an important contribution to American life. The gradual disappearance of restrictions on Jewish life in the colonies also owed much to the spirit of liberty that was marching throughout the land.

CLOSE-UPS: *Prominent Pennsylvanians*

THE GRATZ FAMILY

Barnard (Issachar Ber) Gratz was born in Silesia in Central Europe. When the area was captured by the Prussians, who restricted the rights of the Jews, Barnard came to America by way of London.

Soon after his arrival in Pennsylvania in 1754, Barnard began working for David Franks. From him, he learned about the merchant trade. In 1759 Barnard brought his brother Michael to America, and the two formed a life-long business partnership. They traded along the eastern coast from Canada to the West Indies. With Franks, Joseph Simon of Lancaster, and others, they invested in Western frontier lands and also traded with the Indians.

In 1776 Barnard went to Pittsburgh to negotiate a treaty with the Indians. Michael wrote his brother that he hoped he would get home "before Rosh Hashono, so that you can be with us for the Holidays." Barnard did not think he would make it. He wrote a letter in Yiddish asking that his *maḥzor* (holiday prayer book) be sent to him by the next postrider.

The Gratz brothers were among the founders of the first congregation in Philadelphia, Mikveh Israel. Barnard served as its first *parnas* (president), while Michael was on the board of directors.

Richea (Mrs. Barnard) Gratz

Barnard Gratz

Miriam (Mrs. Michael) Gratz

Michael Gratz

A LANCASTER MERCHANT

In 1732 Joseph Simon opened a general store in Lancaster, Pennsylvania. He became a prosperous merchant and had an outpost in Fort Pitt (Pittsburgh), where he traded land and furs with the Indians. Simon also received large grants of land in what is now Kentucky. To encourage settlement of these lands, he sent traders to supply the goods needed by the colonists.

By 1747 there were ten Jewish families in Lancaster, and Simon's home served as their synagogue. Simon joined with Isaac Nunes Henriques, a refugee from Savannah, to purchase land for a Jewish cemetery. He also gave money for the support of Mikveh Israel congregation in Philadelphia.

The lintel, or stone, above the aron-ha-kodesh (holy ark), in the home of Joseph Simon.

FROM OUR JEWISH HERITAGE:
The Responsibilities of a Jew in a Non-Jewish Land

America is one of the many non-Jewish nations in which the Jews have lived since their exile from the Holy Land. What does our Jewish heritage teach us about some of the special problems facing Jews living in a non-Jewish land?

Exile

When God took Moses up to Mount Nebo, showed him the surrounding countryside and said, "This is the land" (Deuteronomy 34:4), the ancient Hebrews could not have known that most of their descendants would live in exile, far from the land they had been promised. Living outside of the Holy Land has given rise to special problems for the Jewish people. First among them is the need to resist assimilation. The prophets repeatedly warned the people to remain faithful to God and to uphold His laws. "Learn not the way of the nations," said the prophet Jeremiah, "for the customs of the peoples are false." (Jeremiah 10:2-3) If the Jews adopted all of the traditions and laws of the countries in which they lived, worshipped their gods, and intermarried with their peoples, not only would the Jews be sinning against God, but eventually they would be absorbed into the general population and would no longer exist as a distinct people.

The Hebrews in Egypt

According to the Passover *haggadah*, the Hebrews in Egypt "became there a nation, which teaches that the Hebrews were distinctive there." Tradition has it that while in Egypt the Hebrews wore more modest clothing than did the Egyptians, continued to speak Hebrew, and did not give their children the names of Egyptian gods, all of which helped to keep their identity separate from the Egyptians.

Persian Jews

Similarly, much of the biblical story of Esther is a lesson in the struggle against assimilation. When Mordecai refused to bow down to Haman, he was refusing to accept

Haman leads Mordecai through the streets of Shushan. (Esther 6:11)

the customs of the Persian people. Haman complained to King Ahaseurus that there was within his kingdom a group of people who were not the same as the other citizens. "Their laws are different from those of every other people, and they do not keep the king's laws," Haman said. (Esther 3:8) Throughout history, enemies like Haman have tried to destroy the Jewish people because they would not conform. The strength of the Jewish people has been that, through their faithfulness to God and His laws, they have survived for generations even though they were "scattered abroad and dispersed." (Esther 3:8)

Prayer for the Government

Although the Bible frequently orders Jews to preserve their heritage, it also advises them to "seek the welfare of the city where I have sent you into exile, and pray to the Lord on its behalf, for in its welfare you will find your welfare." (Jeremiah 29:7) Following this biblical teaching, a prayer for the

Jews have offered prayers for the American government since revolutionary times. This prayer, read by Gershom Seixas in 1782, asked God's help for "His Excellency the President & Hon'ble Delegates of the United States of America in Congress Assembled, His Excellency George Washington, Captain General & Commander in Chief of the federal Army of these States, His Excellency the President, the Hon'ble the Executive Council & Members of the General Assembly of this Commonwealth [of Pennsylvania] & all Kings and Potentates in Alliance with North America." Seixas prayed, "May the Supreme King of Kings, through his infinite mercies, save and prosper, the Men of these United States, who are gone forth to War."

welfare of the government is part of the morning service on the Sabbath and festivals. A typical prayer reads:

Heavenly Father, we invoke Thy blessings upon the President of the United States of America, and upon all the leaders of our country. Protect them with Thy mercy and sustain them with Thy good counsel. Inspire them to govern the nation in faithfulness and in truth, and direct them ever to seek the welfare of all the inhabitants of our land.

Thou who art the Lord of all mankind, implant within our hearts a respect for law, and a resoluteness of purpose in advancing the cause of freedom, justice and peace. Prosper our country in all her worthy endeavors, and help her to be a force for good among all the nations of the world. Amen. [*The Prayer Book*, translated and arranged by Ben Zion Bokser.]

Marchers in an Israel Day Parade carry American and Israeli flags. American Jews are both loyal to the United States and concerned about the State of Israel.

II · THE AMERICAN REVOLUTION

וּזְעַקְתֶּם בַּיּוֹם הַהוּא מִלִּפְנֵי מַלְכְּכֶם.

"And you will cry out in that day because of your king."
I Samuel 8:18

The Bible tells us that the Israelites came to Samuel, their judge and prophet, and said to him, "Set up for us a king to judge us like all the nations." Samuel cautioned that a king might do unpleasant things to his subjects, such as

Above: The Birth of the Flag, *by the Jewish artist Henry Mosler, shows Betsy Ross and her friends sewing the first American flag.*

drafting them into an army or taxing them. He warned that kings often overstep their powers and become oppressive. Take a king over you, Samuel predicted, and some day you will regret it. "And you will cry out in that day because of your king." (I Samuel 8:5-18)

That is what was happening in eighteenth-century America. The colonists were becoming increasingly rebellious against the rule of the British king, George III. They resented the restrictions on colonial trade set by the British Parliament. They resisted the numerous taxes imposed upon them. Finally, in April 1775, shots were fired at Lexington and Concord and a smouldering rebellion broke into open revolt.

During the colonial era the Jews had been fighting for their personal freedom. Now, together with other colonists, they turned their attention to the battle for the nation's freedom from Great Britain. Most Jews became revolutionaries. By the time the thirteen colonies had won their independence, the Jews were Americans.

The opening lines of the Declaration of Independence.

CHAPTER ONE
THE SPIRIT OF REVOLUTION

Taking Sides

A small group of people fought and won the American Revolution. The majority of colonists did not even support the war. About one-third remained faithful to the British king. These people were called "Loyalists" or "Tories," named after the ruling political party in Britain. Another third were neutral or had no opinion. Only about one-third of the colonists favored the idea of an independent United States. They called themselves "Patriots" or "Whigs" (after the opposition party in Britain).

Loyalty to the Crown

The colonial Jews had always been loyal to the British king, and with good reason. Their life in the British colonies was better than it had been in Europe. They had been allowed to settle in most of the colonies, to worship freely, and, eventually, to build their synagogues. The passage by the British Parliament of the 1740 Naturalization Act had been a landmark for the Jews. It freed them to participate legally in the prosperous colonial trade, and many Jews such as Jacob Rivera, Jacob Franks, and the Gratz brothers did so to great personal advantage.

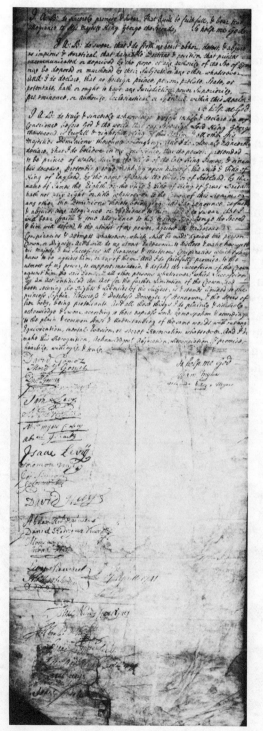

This oath of loyalty to the British king, George II, was signed in 1741, the year after the passage of the Naturalization Act. Most, if not all, of the signers were Jewish. Among them were: David Gomez, Mordecai Gomez, Daniel Gomez, Abraham Myers Cohen, Isaac Levy, Joseph Simson, David Hays, Moses Lopez, Isaac Nunes Henriques, and Hyam Myers.

America's Jews and Christians

There were few incidents of anti-Semitism in the colonies, and many business and personal relationships developed between Christians and Jews. Isaac da Costa, a leader of the Charleston Jewish community, was in partnership with Thomas Farr. Jacob Rivera of Newport formed a business association with numerous Christian members, including John Brown of Providence, one of the founders of Brown University. The Gratz brothers and Joseph Simon of Pennsylvania bought frontier land with Christian partners.

"The Jew Bill"

Even though the freedom enjoyed by Jews in America was greater than in Europe, there were still limits. For example, in colonies such as Pennsylvania, they were not permitted to hold political office. The colonial Jews were also aware that Jews in Great Britain had failed to win equal rights. In 1753 a Jewish Naturalization Bill had been passed by Parliament. The law's purpose was to give foreign-born Jews living in Great Britain limited rights, such as the right to buy property. Opposition to this law led to an outbreak of anti-Semitism in Great Britain and the law was repealed.

Colonial Christians and Jews often gave money to support each other's houses of worship. Among the prominent Philadelphia Christians on this 1788 list of donors to Mikveh Israel are Benjamin Franklin, David Rittenhouse, and Thomas McKean, a signer of the Declaration of Independence.

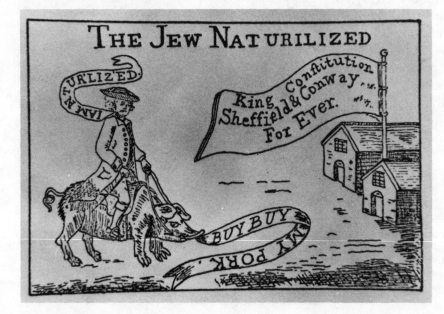

A political cartoon from 1753 concerning the Jewish Naturalization Bill, which stirred up much anti-Jewish feeling in England.

When they heard about this, colonial Jews could not help but be concerned. If the Jewish Naturalization Bill in Great Britain could be revoked, could the Naturalization Act of 1740 relating to colonial Jews also be repealed? Why, many Jews wondered, should they risk a possible loss of hard-won rights by remaining under British rule? After all, the Declaration of Independence insisted that "all men are created equal." In an independent United States, many Jews sensed, they would have greater personal and political freedom than they had ever known in a non-Jewish land.

Jewish Merchants and British Taxes

In addition to the political reasons, there were economic reasons why the Jews favored the Revolution. Many of the colonial Jews were merchants, traders, and shopkeepers. The British taxes on trade and the restrictions on imports threatened their businesses. For this reason, Jews joined other colonists protesting these laws by signing agreements not to import British goods.

A drawing of the time shows the Declaration of Independence being read to the people.

A drawing from the colonial era shows merchants signing the non-importation agreements. Of the 375 merchants who signed the Philadelphia agreement in October, 1765, nine were Jews. They were: Michael and Barnard Gratz, David Franks, Mathias Bush, Benjamin Levy, Samson Levy, Hyman Levy, Jr., Joseph Jacobs, and Moses Mordecai. The New York non-importation agreement of 1770 had about a dozen Jewish signers, including Jonas Phillips, Hayman Levy, Isaac Seixas, Jacob Moses, Manuel Josephson, Uriah Hendricks, Abraham Jacobs, Daniel Jacobs, Samuel Judah, and Jacob Myers.

This cartoon, from revolutionary times, shows rebels hanging a stuffed dummy that represents the hated tax collector.

British taxes were so heavy that men such as the Gratz brothers and Aaron Lopez joined other colonists who engaged in smuggling to avoid paying the import taxes. Perhaps these devout Jews were aware of the teaching of the Talmud that if a king demands unjustly high taxes, this is royal robbery and the taxes may be evaded.

Jewish Patriots

After the revolutionary war, Jonas Phillips, a leader of the Philadelphia Jewish community, wrote:

> The Jews have been true and faithful whigs, & during the late Contest with England they have been foremost in aiding and assisting the states with their lifes & fortunes. [Herbert Friendenwald, "A Letter of Jonas Phillips to the Federal Convention," *AJHQ*]

This was not strictly accurate, as there were also Jewish Loyalists and Jews who chose neither side. However, of the Jews who expressed their views, especially among those who were foreign-born and had no reason to be loyal to the British king, the majority supported the rebel cause.

CLOSE-UPS: *America's Christians and Jews*

THE MASONS

During colonial and revolutionary times, Jews and Christians met as equals at gatherings of the Society of Masons. Masonry was a secret society that claimed to be descended from the craft unions that helped build King Solomon's Temple in Jerusalem. Over the centuries it became a social organization.

Christian patriots who were Masons included George Washington, Benjamin Franklin, and Paul Revere. Some colonial Jews were also members and officers of the Masons, including Moses Seixas, Jonas Phillips, Isaac da Costa, Abraham Alexander, Benjamin Nones, Isaac Franks, Michael Gratz, Haym Salomon, and Benjamin Sheftall.

In 1790, George Washington paid a visit to Newport, Rhode Island. He was welcomed by Moses Seixas, president of Yeshuat Israel synagogue and head of the city's Masonic lodge. Seixas greeted the President as a "brother", or fellow mason. Using the secret passwords of the society, he said, "Permit us then, illustrious brother, cordially to salute you with Three times Three . . ." Washington replied that he was pleased to be welcomed by the Masons and that he would "always be happy to advance the interest of the Society and be considered by them as a deserving Brother."

A CHRISTIAN GUEST DESCRIBES A JEWISH WEDDING

Colonial Christians and Jews often socialized together. In 1787, Dr. Benjamin Rush, who had signed the Declaration of Independence, was a guest at the wedding of Rachel, daughter of Jonas and Rebecca Phillips. In a letter to his wife, Rush wrote about the ceremony, which sounds remarkably similar to a modern Jewish wedding.

The ceremony began with prayers in the Hebrew language, chaunted [chanted] by an old rabbi. . . . A small piece of parchment was produced, written in Hebrew, which contained a deed of settlement [a *ketubah*, the Jewish wedding contract, actually written in Aramaic] and which the groom subscribed in the presence of four witnesses. . . . This was followed by the erection of a beautiful canopy [the hupah] of white and red silk. . . . The bride, accompanied with . . . a long train of female relatives, came downstairs. Her face was covered with a veil which reached halfways down her body.

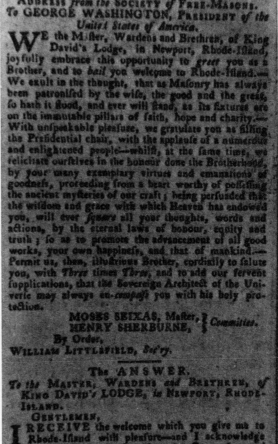

The speeches of fellow Masons, Moses Seixas and George Washington, were printed in The Providence Gazette and Country Journal.

The Christian guest: Dr. Benjamin Rush.

. . . Two young men led the bridegroom . . . directly opposite to her. The priest now began again to chaunt [chant] an Hebrew prayer. . . . After this he gave to the groom and bride a glass full of wine, from which they each sipped . . . after which he took a ring and directed the groom to place it upon the finger of his bride. . . . This was followed by handing the wine to the father of the bride and then . . . to the bride and groom. The groom after sipping the wine took the glass . . . and threw it upon a large pewter dish. . . . Upon its breaking into a number of small pieces, there was a general shout of joy and a declaration that the ceremony was over. [L. H. Butterfield, editor, *The Letters of Benjamin Rush*]

The Jewish bride: Rachel Phillips (Mrs. Michael) Levy.

A drawing of Walter Scott's Rebecca in an old edition of his book, Ivanhoe.

REBECCA GRATZ AND INTER-MARRIAGE

Both because there were not many Jews in the colonies and because there were few social barriers between Christians and Jews, about one in every three Jews married a Christian. Most of the children of these marriages were lost to Judaism.

Some Jews decided to be alone rather than wed a Christian. The most famous of these was Rebecca, daughter of Michael and Miriam Gratz of Philadelphia. A beautiful and charming woman, she was said to be the inspiration for the character of Rebecca in Walter Scott's book, *Ivanhoe*.

Rebecca was deeply in love with Samuel Ewing, a young lawyer and son of a prominent Christian family in Philadelphia. It was said that they did not marry because of their religious differences. Rebecca never married. She once wrote that she believed it was "impossible to reconcile a matrimonial engagement between persons of so different a creed, without requiring one or the other to yield."

Rebecca Gratz devoted her life to charitable work. She was a founder of the Female Association for the Relief of Women and Children in Reduced Circumstances, the Orphan Society, the Hebrew Benevolent Society, the Hebrew Sunday School Society, and other Philadelphia communal associations, on whose behalf she was a tireless worker and fundraiser.

Rebecca Gratz

Religious Liberty, *by the nineteenth century Jewish sculptor, Moses Jacob Ezekiel.*

"ALL MEN ARE CREATED EQUAL"

What did the founding fathers mean when they wrote in the Declaration of Independence that "all men are created equal?"

First of all, "all men" did not mean "all men and women." There were many restrictions on women in the eighteenth century. For example, there were limits on their right to own property and they were not allowed to vote. It was not until the twentieth century that women achieved political equality with men.

Second, the phrase "all men" did not include slaves. Some of the founders owned slaves, had no intention of freeing them, and did not regard them as their equals. "All men" really meant "all free men."

Third, "created equal" did not mean that the founders thought that all people are born with exactly the same qualities. Some people are "created" taller than others, some with brown hair and others with blond. "Created equal" meant that all people are born with the right to be treated equally under the law.

The Declaration's statement that "all men are created equal" and the Constitution's promise of freedom of religion must be seen in light of the religious life of the colonies. Each colony was dominated by a particular Christian religious group: Catholics in Maryland, Congregationalists in Massachusetts, Baptists in Rhode Island, Anglicans in Virginia, and so on. Each of the founders wanted to make sure that the rights of his own religious group would be guaranteed. Most were not broad-minded men who aimed to give religious freedom to everyone. But fortunately for Jews and for all Americans, the words "all men are created equal" eventually came to mean equality for all people, men and women, black and white, under the law.

Left: The signing of the Declaration of Independence. Right: A statue of the Declaration's author, Thomas Jefferson, by Moses Jacob Ezekiel.

FROM OUR JEWISH HERITAGE:
Jewish and American Law

American revolutionaries often compared themselves to the Hebrews of the Bible. The Hebrews were oppressed by Pharoah, the colonists by George III. The Hebrews became a nation when they were brought out of bondage in Egypt, the Americans at the time of the Revolution. And just as there are parallels between Jewish and American history, there are also ways in which Jewish and American law are similar.

Two Peoples of the Book

The Jewish people have long been known as "the people of the book" because of their devotion to the Bible. The Torah, the first five books of the Bible, is the fountain of Jewish law. At the same time this written Torah was revealed to Moses at Sinai, an oral Torah was also given to him. The oral Torah is also a basic part of Jewish law. It helps the people to understand the words of the written Torah.

The oral Torah was finally written down in the Talmud. Other examples of oral Torah are found in the commentaries, decisions, opinions, and writings of the rabbis and scholars who lived after the Talmudic era, such as Maimonides and Rashi.

One could say that Americans are also a "people of the book." Our "written Torah" is the United States Constitution. Our "oral Torah" may be found in the laws that have been passed by federal and state governments; the courtroom arguments, legal papers, and articles on the law by lawyers and scholars; and the decisions by judges.

A print of Moses with the ten commandments, by Seymour Rosenthal.

The Letter of the Law

We are forbidden to change the words of the written Torah. "You shall not add to the word which I command you, nor take from it." (Deuteronomy 4:2) The rabbis teach us that each word of God is like a hammer that breaks a rock into many pieces. Just as a hammer hitting a rock sends out numerous sparks, so each of God's words has seventy interpretations. So although the words of the written Torah cannot be changed, the oral Torah shows us how to understand the many meanings of each word in the written Torah.

Similarly, changing the words of the Constitution is so difficult that it is almost impossible. There are only two ways it can be done. The first is to call a constitutional convention. Only one constitutional convention has been held in the history of this country. That was the very first one, which resulted in our present Constitution.

The other way to change the Constitution is through an *amendment*, a change that must be accepted by three-fourths of all the state governments. This is a very difficult process. In fact there have been only twenty-six amendments since the Constitution was first written.

The American Constitution changes slowly, but it does grow. It changes as judges,

The Liberty Bell in Philadelphia, with the inscription "Proclaim liberty throughout the land, unto all the inhabitants thereof." The words are from Leviticus 25:10.

lawyers, and lawmakers apply it to new problems and situations. Its words may stay the same, but people understand them in new ways.

Both Jewish and American law are based on an unchanging code of written laws, yet are constantly changing. Both systems are alive and growing! One can see this by looking at how each deals with modern inventions, such as the telephone, that did not exist when the laws were written.

Benjamin Franklin, Thomas Jefferson, and John Adams favored a design like this one for the official seal of the United States. The seal shows the Egyptians drowning in the Red Sea while the children of Israel watch safely from the other shore. It is typical of the feeling of the American revolutionaries that their situation was like that of the Hebrews in Egypt.

An Example from Jewish Law

According to Jewish law, you are not supposed to kindle a fire on Shabbat. The literal meaning of the law is clear: don't light a fire. The oral Torah interprets this law far more broadly. It prohibits starting anything that gives light or heat. In modern times, this law has been extended to anything that produces an electric spark. On Shabbat, observant Jews do not turn on the television, ride in cars, or use the telephone. According to the oral Torah, all would involve breaking the written Torah's commandment not to kindle a fire.

An Example from American Law

The Fourth Amendment of the U.S. Constitution protects people from "unreasonable searches and seizures" of their persons, houses, papers, etc. This means that the police can't do such things as go through your closets or open your mail without a search warrant. What about your telephone conversations? Can the police listen in when you are talking on the phone, or would that be an "unreasonable search and seizure?"

Judges, lawyers, and legal scholars have argued about this question, knowing that there were no telephones in 1787, when the Constitution was written. They decided that the "search and seizure" clause of the Constitution also protects the privacy of telephone conversations. As a result, if the police want to tap your phone, they usually need a search warrant.

Right: The Journal of Halacha and Contemporary Society, *a magazine dedicated to the study of twentieth century questions in light of Jewish law and values.*

The Spirit of the Law

By understanding the many meanings behind the words of their written laws, Jewish rabbis and American lawyers have been able to figure out what to do about new inventions such as the telephone. They look at the words of the written laws, and instead of changing them, they see them in a new light. In this way, both the Jewish and American legal systems have continued to grow and develop as they respond to the needs of the modern world.

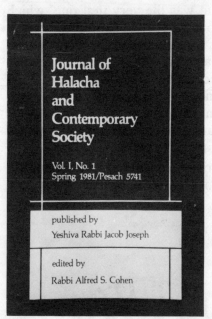

The United States Constitution.

CHAPTER TWO

THE WAR IN THE NORTH

Wartime Refugees

At the time of the revolutionary war, five American cities had organized Jewish communities: Newport, New York, and Philadelphia in the North, and Savannah and Charleston in the South. As each of these cities was captured by the British, many citizens, including Jews, were forced to flee. Jewish community life was disrupted by the war as families moved from one city to another.

Newport

In the summer of 1776, patriotic feelings were strong. The Rhode Island Assembly passed a law requiring any man suspected of British sympathies to take an oath of loyalty to the revolutionary cause. In Newport, seventy-seven men were called upon to take this oath, including four Jews: Isaac Hart, "Parson Tororo Jew Priest" (Isaac Touro, the congregation's leader), Myer Polock, and Moses Michael Hays. All four refused to take the oath. Hart, Touro, and Polock were Loyalists. Hays, however, was a patriot. He declined to sign the oath as a matter of principle. Eventually, his name was cleared.

Newport was occupied by the British from December 1776 to October 25, 1779. The city's trade was destroyed by the war and most of the citizens who fled did not return. Newport never regained the position of prominence it held during colonial times. In 1790, a few Jews remained to offer a message of welcome to President George Washington when he visited the city. By 1822 there were no Jews in Newport and the synagogue's Torah scrolls were sent to Shearith Israel in New York.

The house and store of Aaron Lopez in Leicester, Massachusetts, where the Lopez family lived after the British captured Newport.

CLOSE-UPS: *Newport in Revolutionary Times*

Isaac Touro

Edmund Burke, the famous British writer and politician, asked Parliament to compensate Polock and Hart for the losses they had suffered during the war. Burke argued that because Polock "had imported tea contrary to the command of the Americans, he was stripped of all he was worth" and driven from Newport.

Moses Michael Hays

NEWPORT'S JEWISH LOYALISTS

Three of Newport's Jews refused to take an oath of loyalty to the rebel cause. They were Meyer Polock, Isaac Hart, and Isaac Touro, leader of the local synagogue.

Touro and his family left Newport for New York, where he received a pension from the British. In 1782, the Touros went to Jamaica. When her husband died the next year, Reyna Hays Touro and her children went to Boston to live with her brother, Moses Michael Hays.

Isaac Hart and Myer Polock were both Tories with close business ties to the British. In 1780 Hart was deprived of all rights and property by the Rhode Island Assembly because of his Tory sympathies. He went to New York and the British gave him some land on Long Island. Hart was killed while fighting for the British at Fort George. According to a newspaper account, he was "inhumanely fired upon and bayonetted" fifteen times.

A battle scene of the American Revolution, drawn by an artist of that time.

A MAN OF PRINCIPLE

Moses Michael Hays refused to take the loyalty oath because he felt that individual liberty was at stake. He argued that he was being convicted of disloyalty without a trial. He said that as a Jew he could not vote in Rhode Island. Why, he asked, should he have the responsibilities of citizenship without its privileges? Hays pointed out that the Continental Congress and legislatures of other states had also failed to ensure the rights of Jews. Finally, he said that requiring an oath of only some of Newport's citizens was unfair. This last argument was accepted, and eventually all men were asked to take the oath.

With the wartime decline of Newport, Hays moved to Boston. He became a great success in the insurance business and a prominent member of the Masons. According to the Protestant minister, Samuel J. May, Hays was "a man much respected, not only on account of his large wealth, but for his many personal virtues." May said that poor people "were fed pretty regularly from his table," especially on Shabbat, when he always "expected a number of friends to dine with him." The Hays family may have been the only Jews living in Boston at that time.

A MESSAGE FROM PRESIDENT WASHINGTON

On behalf of the remaining Jews in the congregation of Yishuat Yisrael, Moses Seixas welcomed President George Washington to Newport in 1790. Seixas said:

> Deprived as we [Jews] hitherto have been of the invaluable rights of free citizens, we now—with a deep sense of gratitude to the Almighty Disposer of all events—behold a government erected by the majesty of the people—a government which to bigotry gives no sanction, to persecution no assistance, but generously affording to all liberty of conscience and immunities of citizenship, deeming every one of whatever nation, tongue, or language, equal parts of the great governmental machine.

Washington replied that in this country,

> All possess alike liberty of conscience and immunities of citizenship. . . . May the Children of the Stock of Abraham, who dwell in this land, continue to merit and enjoy the good will of the other Inhabitants, while every one shall sit in safety under his own vine and fig tree, and there shall be none to make him afraid.

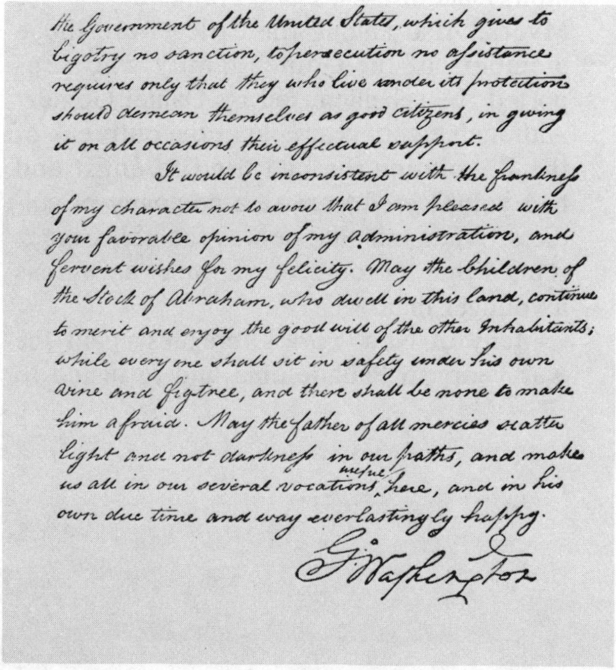

This last thought was taken from the text of Micah 4:4.

The Jewish congregations in New York, Philadelphia, Charleston, Richmond, and Savannah also sent messages of congratulation to the President and received similar replies.

To the Hebrew Congregation in Newport
Rhode Island.

Gentlemen.

While I receive, with much satisfaction, your Address replete with expressions of affection and esteem; I rejoice in the opportunity of assuring you, that I shall always retain a grateful remembrance of the cordial welcome I experienced in my visit to Newport, from all classes of Citizens.

The reflection on the days of difficulty and danger which are past is rendered the more sweet, from a consciousness that they are succeeded by days of uncommon prosperity and security. If we have wisdom to make the best use of the advantages with which we are now favored, we cannot fail, under the just administration of a good Government, to become a great and a happy people.

The Citizens of the United States of America have a right to applaud themselves for having given to mankind examples of an enlarged and liberal policy: a policy worthy of imitation. All possess alike liberty of conscience and immunities of citizenship. It is now no more that toleration is spoken of, as if it was by the indulgence of one class of people, that another enjoyed the exercise of their inherent natural rights. For happily the

the Government of the United States, which gives to bigotry no sanction, to persecution no assistance requires only that they who live under its protection should demean themselves as good citizens, in giving it on all occasions their effectual support.

It would be inconsistent with the frankness of my character not to avow that I am pleased with your favorable opinion of my administration, and fervent wishes for my felicity. May the Children of the Stock of Abraham, who dwell in this land, continue to merit and enjoy the good will of the other Inhabitants; while every one shall sit in safety under his own vine and figtree, and there shall be none to make him afraid. May the father of all mercies scatter light and not darkness in our paths, and make us all in our several vocations useful here, and in his own due time and way everlastingly happy.

G Washington

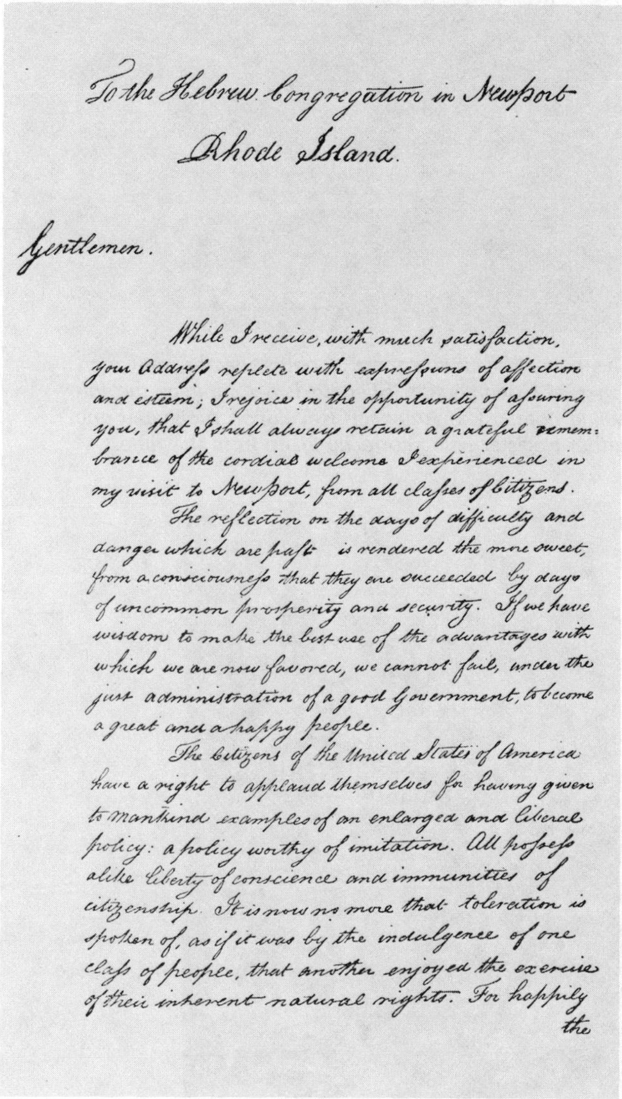

President Washington's letter to the Newport congregation.

New York

The city was captured in 1776 by British forces. Some thousand New York citizens took an oath of loyalty to King George III, including sixteen Jews. These Jewish Loyalists remained in New York throughout the occupation. So did most of those who could not afford to leave or those who had no relatives in other cities with whom they could seek shelter.

Many of the members of Shearith Israel followed the example of their religious leader, Gershom Mendes Seixas, who urged that they leave New York. Among those who did were Jonas Phillips, Haym Salomon, Isaac Moses, Isaac Franks, and Myer Myers. Also among the exiles were those members of the Gomez family who supported the rebellion, led by Daniel Gomez. Although eighty years old at the outbreak of the Revolution, he had tried to enlist and had volunteered to raise a company of soldiers. When told that he was too old, Gomez replied that he could stop a bullet as well as a younger man.

Many of New York's refugees spent the war years in Philadelphia and returned to New York in 1783, when the hostilities ceased. The Minute Book of Shearith Israel contains the following entry in 1783:

During the interval [from 1776 to 1783] most of the Yehadim [Jews] had left the city in consequence of the Revolutionary War and the city having been taken possession of by the British troops, it was not until peace took place that the members returned to the city, when Mr. Hayman Levy called the meeting. [Shearith Israel Archives]

This page from the register of births, deaths, and marriages of Congregation Shearith Israel contains the following note: "The American Revolution prevented any further Register being correctly taken from this time."

Washington's entry into New York after the British evacuated, November 25, 1783.

CLOSE-UPS: *New York Patriots*

Statue of Robert Morris, George Washington, and Haym Salomon on Wacker Drive in Chicago.

A REBEL FINANCIER

Haym Salomon was a Polish immigrant living in New York when it was captured by the British. He was arrested on suspicion of being a spy, but was released when it was discovered that he spoke German. The British put him to work as an interpreter for the Hessians, German-speaking soldiers fighting for the British.

In 1778 he escaped to Philadelphia where he went into business as a broker dealing in money, notes, and bills of exchange. He was named a broker to the rebel Office of Finance and worked with its superintendent, Robert Morris, to raise funds for the revolutionary government. According to Morris, Salomon was "useful to the public Interest."

Salomon also made personal loans to many of the founding fathers, including James Madison, General Arthur St. Clair, Baron von Steuben, Thaddeus Kosciuszko, General Thomas Mifflin, and Edmund Randolph. Madison wrote to Randolph that Salomon "rejects all recompense. . . . To a necessitous delegate [to the revolutionary Congress] he gratuitously spares a supply out of his private stock."

Salomon charged a commission of ½ percent per transaction, much less than the 2–5 percent charged by other brokers. His faith in the Revolution was such that he invested most of his money in Continental stocks and bonds.

A charitable man, Salomon was the largest contributor to the building fund of Mikveh Israel in Philadelphia. Because of this, he had the honor of opening the synagogue's door on the day of its dedication. He also supported numerous relatives in Europe. He advised them not to come to America because there was *"vaynig yiddishkeit"* (little Jewishness) here.

Haym Solomons,

BROKER to the Office of Finance, to the Consul General of France, and to the Treasurer of the French Army, at his Office in Front-street, between Market and Arch-streets, BUYS and SELLS on Commission

BANK Stock, Bills of Exchange on France, Spain, Holland, and other parts of Europe, the West Indies, and inland bills, at the usual commission.——He Buys and Sells

Loan-Office Certificates, Continental and State Money, of this or any other state, Paymaster and Quartermaster Generals Notes; these and every other kind of paper transactions (bills of exchange excepted) he will charge his employers no more than ONE HALF PER CENT on his Commission,

He procures Money on Loan for a short time, and gets Notes and Bills discounted.

Gentlemen and others, residing in this state, or any of the united states, by sending their orders to this Office, may depend on having their business transacted with as much fidelity and expedition, as if they were themselves present.

He receives Tobacco, Sugars, Tea, and every other sort of Goods to Sell on Commission; for which purpose he has provided proper Stores.

He flatters himself, his assiduity, punctuality, and extensive connections in his business, as a Broker, is well established in various parts of Europe, and in the united states in particular.

All persons who shall please to favour him with their business, may depend upon his utmost exertion for their interest, and——

Part of the Money advanced, if required.

N. B. Paymaster-General's Notes taken as Cash for Bills of Exchange.

Salomon's advertisement in a Philadelphia newspaper names him as "Broker to the Office of Finance."

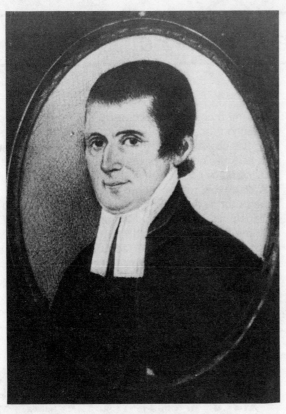

Gershom Mendes Seixas

BURNING THE FARM OF PATRIOTS

David and Esther Hays had a farm and store in Bedford, New York. They supported the Revolution. Once David gave his daughter a *siddur* [prayer book] that had a prayer for the government. So strongly did David hate the British that he crossed out the prayers for the welfare of King George III and his family.

In 1779 David was fighting in the rebel army. When their men went off to battle, farm women like Esther Hays were left to work the land and protect themselves and their children. The Hays farm was also being used to store food and supplies for the Continental army.

Esther was still in bed recovering from the birth of her son when a group of local Loyalists came to her home. They demanded to know the rebels' plans. When Esther refused to tell them anything, they set her house on fire. Esther and her children and servants escaped to the woods.

The Hays family was close-knit and traditional. In letters to his brother Michael, David sent his best wishes for a "good *Shabos*," reminded him of their mother's *yahrtzeit* (anniversary of death), and invited him to "come & keep Yomtob [Jewish holiday] with us."

THE REFUGEE RABBI

Gershom Mendes Seixas was the first American-born religious leader of a Jewish congregation and the first to give sermons in English. Seixas was born in New York in 1745, and was appointed *hazan* of Shearith Israel in 1768. When the British captured New York, Seixas fled to Connecticut. In 1780 he went to Philadelphia where he helped to organize construction of the Mikveh Israel synagogue and served as its first religious leader.

In one of his many patriotic wartime sermons, Seixas prayed that God would

> bless, guard, preserve, assist, shield, Save, supremely Exalt, and aggrandize to a high degree . . . His Excellency George Washington, Capt. Genl. & Commander in Chief of the Federal Army of these States. . . . [May] the supreme King of kings through his infinite mercies, save and prosper the Men of these United States, who are gone forth to War. . . . We Beeseech thee, O Most gracious and Merciful king, to whom peace Pertaineth, that thou wilt cause us to enjoy firm Peace and Tranquility. . . . [Mikveh Israel Archives]

After the war Seixas returned to New York and resumed his post as leader of Shearith Israel. In 1789 he was one of thirteen clergymen who participated in the inauguration of George Washington as the nation's first president.

Left alone by husbands who went to war, women often found themselves in the middle of battle.

Philadelphia

Like the other Jewish communities, Philadelphia had its share of wartime heroes. These included David Salisbury Franks, Benjamin Nones, and Solomon Bush. Bush fought in the battles of Long Island and Brandywine and was made a lieutenant colonel, the highest rank achieved by a Jew in the combat forces of the Continental Army. Philadelphia was also the home of one of the most well known Jewish Loyalists, David Franks.

Philadelphia became rebel headquarters during the war after the British left in 1778. The city's Jews witnessed many historic scenes, from the entrance of the delegates to the First Continental Congress in 1774 to the 1788 parade celebrating the ratification of the United States Constitution. As the wartime national capital, Philadelphia was also the center of another Jewish contribution to the Revolution: participation in the economic activities that financed the war.

Financing the Revolution

Jews helped raise funds to support the rebellion by signing bills of credit for the Continental Congress; acting as brokers for the Continental Office of Finance; and lending money to the states. Jewish merchants, including the Sheftall and Minis families of Georgia, the Gratz brothers of Philadelphia, and David Salisbury Franks of Montreal, provided supplies to the Continental forces. Joseph Simon manufactured flintlock rifles for Washington's army. Myer Myers, a silversmith, melted down metal household goods and turned them into bullets. Men such as Mordecai Sheftall and Isaac Moses helped outfit privateers and armed ships that ran past the British blockades to bring much-needed goods to the war-torn colonies.

Many of these merchants advanced their own funds to pay for supplies, often receiving no repayment. Some accepted paper money rather than gold or silver, even though they knew that the Continental currency was of little value. By the end of the war, many Jewish businessmen were bankrupt, including Michael Gratz, Haym Salomon, and Aaron Lopez. For those motivated only by hopes of making money, these losses were just bad luck. For others, the risks taken were their personal contributions to the future of America.

With the financial and organizational help of the wartime refugees, Philadelphia's first synagogue building was dedicated in 1782. When peace came, many Jews who had spent the war years in Philadelphia returned to their hometowns. It was not until the nineteenth century that the Philadelphia Jewish community again numbered as many as it had during the Revolution.

Left: Isaac Moses financed ships that ran the British blockades and brought needed supplies to the rebels. In payment, he accepted paper money that was worthless after the war. Right: Simon Nathan lent large sums of money to the Virginia state government and suffered great losses when he was not repaid.

CLOSE-UPS: *Philadelphia Personalities*

DAVID SALISBURY FRANKS

David Salisbury Franks was born in Philadelphia and went to Montreal as a merchant. His anti-British feelings led to his name appearing on a list of "the principal leaders of sedition." When the American army attacked the British in Canada, Franks helped to supply it. "My good offices and purse were ever open to them," he later wrote, "at a time when they had neither friend nor money."

Franks returned to America with the invading forces and became an aide to General Benedict Arnold. After Arnold was found guilty of treason, Franks was cleared of any participation in Arnold's crimes. It was found that Frank's conduct

> reflects the highest honor on him as an officer, distinguishes him as a zealous friend to the independence of America, and justly entitles him to the attention and confidence of his countrymen. [Samuel Rezneck, *Unrecognized Patriots: The Jews in the American Revolution*]

Franks left the army with the rank of lieutenant colonel. In 1784 he was one of three messengers sent to Europe with copies of the treaty that ended the Revolutionary War.

Jacob Mordecai

JACOB MORDECAI

Jacob Mordecai was born in Philadelphia, son of Moses Mordecai and Elizabeth (Esther) Whitlock, a Christian convert to Judaism. In 1774, when Jacob was a twelve-year-old schoolboy, he and his friends were armed with guns and given military training. They participated in the parade honoring the delegates to the First Continental Congress. As Jacob described it,

> The road was lined with people, and resounded with huzzas, drums, etc. and exhibited a lively scene. In the humble office of sergeant I had thus the honor of escorting into Philadelphia the first American Congress. [Gratz Mordecai: "Notice of Jacob Mordecai," *PAJHS* 1897]

Jacob became a merchant and he also opened a famous school for women in North Carolina, the Warrenton Female Academy. In 1819 he moved to Richmond, Virginia, where he was a president of that city's first synagogue, Beth Shalome.

David Salisbury Franks

BENJAMIN NONES

Benjamin Nones came from France to fight for this country's freedom. He was on Lafayette's staff and fought with Pulaski's legion in defense of Charleston. A fellow officer said of him that "his behavior under fire in all the bloody battles we fought has been marked by . . . bravery and courage. . . ."

After the war Nones settled in Philadelphia where he became a major in the Pennsylvania militia, served as

President of Mikveh Israel, and was active in Republican party politics. When a political opponent attacked him by making anti-Semitic remarks, Nones defended himself in a newspaper article:

> I am accused of being a Jew. . . . I glory in belonging to that persuasion. I am poor; I am so, my family is also large, but soberly and decently brought up. They have not been taught to revile a Christian because his religion is not as old as theirs. They have not been taught to mock at conscientious belief. [*The Philadelphia Aurora*, Aug. 13, 1800]

Benjamin Nones

Isaac Franks

ISAAC FRANKS

Isaac Franks was born in New York, son of Sarah and Moses Franks and brother of Rachel, wife of Haym Salomon. At the age of seventeen he enlisted in Colonel Lasher's Volunteers in New York. Franks fought on Long Island and was captured when the British took New York. After spending three months in prison, he escaped to New Jersey, rejoined Washington's army, and became its forage (supplies) master.

After the war, Franks was made a colonel in the Pennsylvania militia. In 1793 he rented his house in Germantown (outside of Philadelphia) to President Washington, so that Washington and his family could escape the yellow fever epidemic that was sweeping through the city.

Franks' home, which was rented to President Washington.

JONAS AND REBECCA PHILLIPS

German-born Jonas Phillips arrived in Charleston in 1756 as a servant of Moses Lindo. He died in 1803, a rich merchant, an American patriot, and a leader of the Jewish community.

A supporter of the Revolution, Phillips signed the New York non-importation agreement of 1770. When the British threatened New York, he and his family went to Philadelphia. In 1778 he enlisted as a private in the Pennsylvania militia.

Phillips sent a letter about religious freedom to the Constitutional Convention of 1787. He noted that during the Revolution Jews had "bravely fought and bled for liberty." Yet in some states, he said, Jews could not hold political office. Phillips said that the United States should be a nation "where all Religious societys are on an Equal footing."

Phillips' wife, Rebecca, helped raise money for congregation Mikveh Israel's first synagogue. She and Grace Seixas Nathan headed the drive to raise money for a silk cloth for the ḥazan's desk, a curtain for the ark, and covers for the Torahs. Phillips and Haym Salomon donated the Torah scrolls and Abraham Mendes Seixas, a refugee from Charleston, gave a silver cup for *havdalah*, the ceremony marking the end of Shabbat.

Jonas Phillips

Rebecca Machado Phillips

WITH WASHINGTON'S ARMY AT VALLEY FORGE

Although Philip Moses Russell of Philadelphia was born in England, he resented the policies of the British king towards the colonies and he supported the patriots in their fight for independence. In 1776, he joined the revolutionary army as a surgeon's mate, an assistant to the regiment's medical officer.

During the winter of 1777–78, Russell served under the direct command of General Washington. The army was camped at Valley Forge, Pennsylvania. Soldiers suffered terribly from hunger, cold, and ill health. Many of them died. Surgeon's mate Russell worked tirelessly tending the sick and wounded. In his weakened condition, he caught a severe fever that left him with a loss of hearing and vision. He remained in the army, but his health got worse and in 1780, he resigned.

General Washington himself wrote Russell a letter commending him on his service to the nation. Although the letter was later lost in a fire, Russell's children often had read it with pride. His son Moses remembered that Washington wrote that Russell had served "with honor to himself and his country and he [Washington] with pleasure bore testimony to his assiduous attention to the sick and wounded as well as his cool and collected deportment in battle."

After the war, Russell returned to Philadelphia, where he worked as a pharmacist.

Philip Moses Russell

Winter at Valley Forge.

David Franks and his sister Phila.

QUEEN OF LOYALIST SOCIETY

Rebecca, the beautiful daughter of David Franks, was openly sympathetic to the British. During their occupation of her home-city of Philadelphia she was declared "Queen of the Knights of the Burning Mountain" at a social event organized by the British. Rebecca married Henry Johnson, a British officer, and returned with him to Britain. Apparently she later regretted her Loyalist leanings. In 1816 she was reported to have said, "I, too, have gloried in my rebel countrymen. . . . Would to God I, too, had been a patriot!"

Rebecca Franks

ON TRIAL FOR TREASON

Although David Franks signed the Philadelphia non-importation agreement in 1765, he was no sympathizer to the rebel cause. Franks had family in London, his sister Phila was married to the Loyalist general Oliver Delancey, and he had close economic ties with the British. During the revolutionary war, with the permission of the rebel government, he served the Crown by providing supplies for British soldiers taken prisoner in America.

In 1779 Franks was arrested and tried for treason. The basis of this charge was a letter he had sent to his brother in London, in which he discussed the war-inflated prices in Philadelphia. He also complained that "People are taken and confined at the pleasure of every scoundrel. Oh, what a situation Britain has left its friends!" After a jury trial, Franks was acquitted.

There was much publicity and continuing doubts about his loyalty. Franks was finally expelled from Philadelphia in 1780, "there being just reason to suspect [he is an] enemy . . . to the American cause." He went to England, where he tried in vain to gain repayment for his services to the king.

THE FEDERAL PARADE OF 1788

In 1788, when the United States Constitution was adopted by the states, a celebration parade was held in Philadelphia. Naphtali, the fifteen-year-old son of Jonas and Rebecca Phillips, was one of the marchers. Years later he wrote about this event:

> First in an open carriage drawn by elegant horses, sat Chief Justice McKane [Thomas McKean] . . . holding in his hand the new Constitution in a frame. This was received by the populace with great rejoicing. . . . Next, a printing press on a platform drawn by horses, compositors setting types; and the press worked by journeymen distributing some printed matter as they went along. . . . Next came blacksmiths with their forge, with a large bellows keeping up a blast to keep alive the flame of liberty. . . . The procession then proceeded . . . towards Bush Hill where there were a number of long tables loaded with all kinds of provisions, with a separate table for the Jews who could not partake of the meals from the other tables [because the food was not kosher]; but they had a full supply of soused salmon, bread and crackers, almonds, raisins, etc. [*American Jewish Archives*, 1955]

Naphtali Phillips

Young Phillips went on to become one of the first Jewish newspaper-publishers in the United States and was the owner of the *National Advocate* in New York.

CHAPTER THREE
REVOLT IN THE SOUTH

Savannah

Georgia was filled with Jewish Patriots. James Wright, the Royal Governor of the colony, reported to London that the Jews "were found to a man to have been violent rebels and persecutors of the King's loyal subjects."

Mordecai Sheftall was chairman of the Parochial Committee, the rebel organization in Savannah. The committee also included Philip Minis. One of the group's aims was to enforce the boycott of British goods that had been ordered by the First Continental Congress. The committee blocked British trade by preventing ships from unloading their cargoes in Savannah. The Royal Governor informed London that

> The conduct of the people here [in Savannah] is most infamous. One Sheftall, a Jew, is chairman of the Parochial Committee, as they call themselves, and this fellow issues orders to captains of vessels to depart the king's port without landing any of their cargoes, legally imported. And fresh insults continue to be offered every day. . . . [Jacob R. Marcus, *American Jewry: Documents*]

Among the committee's most successful "insults" was the removal of gunpowder from one of the ships in the Savannah harbor. The cargo was then sent to Boston for use by Washington's army.

When Savannah fell in 1778, those Jewish Patriots who were not captured by the British fled to Charleston. In 1780 the British passed a law by which they tried to prevent Patriots from returning to Georgia. Listed among the "violent rebels" were Mordecai Sheftall, his son Sheftall Sheftall, his brother Levi Sheftall, Philip Minis, Cushman Polock, and Philip Jacob Cohen.

This congressional letter of recommendation for Cushman Polock, a Georgia patriot, states that he "gave early demonstration of his attachment to the American cause, by taking an active part, has been in several engagements against the enemy, when he behaved himself with approbation."

Charleston

Charleston's Jewish community grew as refugees arrived from Savannah. Jews helped defend the city and a part of the Charleston militia was known as "the Jew Company" because about two dozen of its members were Jewish. Among these were Jacob I. Cohen, Abraham Mendes Seixas (brother of the leader of New York's Shearith Israel), and Isaiah Isaacs, later a founder of Beth Shalome synagogue in Richmond, Virginia. "The Jew Company" fought

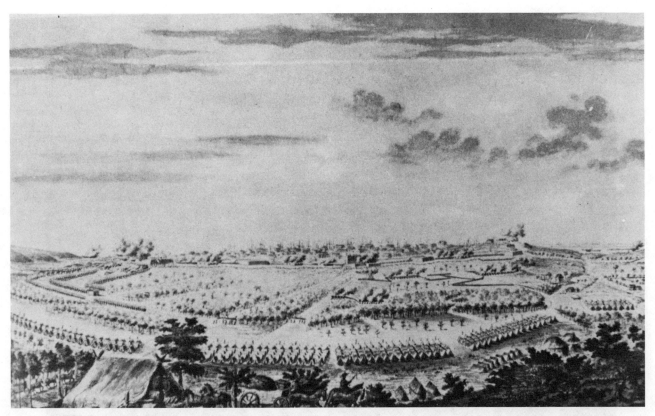

A 1779 drawing of the unsuccessful attempt by French and American forces to recapture Savannah from the British.

in the Battle of Beaufort and was also a part of the force that tried to recapture Savannah in 1779. Savannah natives Philip Minis and Levi Sheftall, then in Charleston, provided maps, information, and guidance to the expedition, but it failed in its mission.

The Battle of Charleston

Among the Savannah refugees who gathered in Charleston were Frances Sheftall and her children. Her husband, Mordecai, and oldest son, Sheftall, were away fighting the British, so Frances found work as a seamstress to support her family. When a smallpox epidemic swept the city, Frances joined other women in helping to nurse the sick and wounded.

The Sheftall family had fled to Savannah hoping to get away from the war, but it soon followed them to Charleston. Frances wrote to her husband of the "continous firing of the cannon on the British warships." One of

these cannonballs killed Rachel, the young daughter of Myer Moses. She may well have been the only Jewish female to die of war wounds.

A 1780 drawing shows a view of the Battle of Charleston from behind British lines.

An eighteenth-century sketch of the Battle of Charleston.

The Fall of Charleston

When the city fell to the British in 1780, Abraham Mendes Seixas and Isaac da Costa were banished because they refused to swear their loyalty to the British king. Like many patriots who escaped from captured cities, they went to Philadelphia.

Charleston grew rapidly after the war. By the early nineteenth century, the city had the largest Jewish community in the United States.

The Impact of the War

In September 1776, Nathan Bush sent a letter to Michael Gratz describing the Battle of Long Island. Bush wrote that "our people retreated." By "our people," Bush was not referring to the Jews, but to the rebel forces. His letter illustrates one of the most important effects of the Revolution on colonial Jews. Before the war, they were a diverse group with varying loyalties, an assortment of European and native-born Jews scattered throughout the thirteen colonies. The war, in which some had given their lives, others their fortunes, had turned them all into Americans. As Mordecai Sheftall wrote to his son, "An entire new scene will open itself, and we have the world to begin again."

CLOSE-UPS: *Southern Patriots*

Sheftall Sheftall

REVOLUTIONARY SHEFTALLS

Mordecai Sheftall was chairman of the Savannah Parochial Committee, a revolutionary organization, and a colonel in the Georgia Brigade. He was also Commissary General for Purchases and Issues of the state militia. Later he was appointed to a similar position for the rebel forces in South Carolina and Georgia. His sixteen-year-old son, Sheftall Sheftall, served as his deputy. The Sheftalls were in charge of obtaining, storing, and issuing supplies to the rebels. They often used their own money for purchases.

When Savannah fell in 1778, both father and son were captured by British forces. They were well-guarded because Mordecai Sheftall was considered "a very great rebel" by the British commander. Mordecai later wrote of his experiences as a prisoner. He said that a British officer asked him to give information on supplies.

This I declined doing, which made him angry. . . . [H]e ordered me to be confined amongst the drunken soldiers and negroes, where I suffered a great deal of abuse and was threatened to be run through the body. . . . I remained two days without a morsel to eat [Sheftall was kosher] when a Hessian officer . . . permitted me to send to Mrs. Minis who sent me some victuals. . . . [Jacob R. Marcus, *Memoirs of American Jews*]

The Sheftalls were released, re-imprisoned, then released again. Eventually they made their way to Philadelphia. In 1780 the younger Sheftall was put in charge of a ship, *The Carolina Packet*, and sent to Charleston under a flag of truce to bring supplies to that war-torn city. After the war the Sheftalls returned to Savannah.

THE REBEL MINIS FAMILY

When Abraham Minis died in 1757, his wife Abigail took over his businesses. By the time of the revolutionary war, she and her children had increased the family's holdings in Georgia to over twenty-five hundred acres. They also had over fifteen slaves, a tavern and a store.

Abigail's son Philip (Uri) was a distinguished Patriot. He was a member of Georgia's Parochial Committee. As acting paymaster and commissary of Georgia's forces, he advanced $11,000 of his own money to the rebel forces so they could purchase supplies.

Philip went to Charleston in 1778, when Savannah was captured by the British. The women of his family remained behind, including his wife, Judith. Although she was the sister of Myer Polock, the Loyalist from Newport, Judith Polock Minis was a Patriot. She was so outspoken a supporter of the Revolution that, to punish her, the British made her work for them as a domestic servant.

In 1779 the Minis women sent a petition to Governor James Wright and the Royal Council of Georgia. They asked permission to go to Charleston because "belonging to the Whig party, they are persecuted." Their request was granted and the women joined Philip in Charleston. The family returned to Savannah after the war.

Judith Polock Minis

Jacob I. Cohen

JACOB I. COHEN

Jacob I. Cohen came to America from Germany in 1773. He joined the Charleston militia and fought in the Battle of Beaufort as a member of "the Jew Company." His commander wrote that "in every respect [he] conducted himself as a good soldier and man of courage."

After the war, Cohen went to Philadelphia. In 1782 he became the center of a religious controversy when he announced his engagement to Esther Mordecai, widow of Moses Mordecai and a convert to Judaism. As a *kohain*, a descendant of the ancient priests of Israel, Cohen was forbidden by Jewish law to marry a convert. The board of directors of Mikveh Israel ordered Gershom Seixas not to conduct the marriage.

Cohen married Esther Mordecai anyway. They moved to Richmond, where Cohen became one of the founders of Beth Shalome synagogue. After his wife's death, he returned to Philadelphia, where he became president of Mikveh Israel Congregation.

ENGLISH ARISTOCRAT AND AMERICAN REBEL

Francis Salvador was born in England to a wealthy and prominent Sephardic family. He came to America to oversee the family's indigo plantation outside of Charleston.

Salvador's uncle Joseph had led the struggle for the Jewish Naturalization Bill of 1753. Perhaps influenced by this failure to win civil liberties for Great Britain's Jews, the young Salvador became an active supporter of the American Patriots' cause. He was a member of both Revolutionary Provincial Congresses in South Carolina and helped write that state's constitution.

When the British and their sympathizers stirred up the Cherokee Indians against the colonists, Salvador joined the militia. On August 1, 1776, his troop was ambushed. Salvador was shot three times. Mortally wounded, he asked his commander whether they had won the battle. When told yes, he said he was very glad of it. Minutes later, he died.

Salvador was probably the first Jewish soldier to give his life in the Revolutionary War. In 1950, a plaque was put up in his honor in Charleston. It reads: "True to his ancient faith, he gave his life for new hopes of human liberty and understanding."

THE FIGHTING *ḤAZAN*

In 1764 Isaac da Costa stepped down as *ḥazan* of Charleston's Beth Elohim synagogue and London-born Abraham Alexander replaced him. When Charleston fell in 1780, Alexander joined rebels fighting outside the city and helped drive the British from the Carolinas. He was a lieutenant in the Light Dragoons, a company in the South Carolina militia headed by Colonel Wade Hampton.

He served as *ḥazan* until 1784, when he resigned after marrying Ann Sara Huguenin Irby, a Protestant by birth. Mrs. Alexander converted to Judaism before her marriage and remained devout throughout her life. In her will, she expressed her belief in "the Almighty God of Israel my Creator."

A Hebrew scholar and *sofer* (scribe), Alexander hand-wrote a *maḥzor* (holiday prayer book) for Rosh Hashanah and Yom Kippur.

Abraham Alexander

The title page of the maḥzor *(holiday prayer book) hand-printed by Alexander.*

FROM OUR JEWISH HERITAGE:
Jews in the Armed Forces

Many Jews were among the patriots who fought the British during the revolutionary war. Ever since Asser Levy first won the right to join the New Amsterdam militia, Jews have continued to serve in the American military. What does our Jewish heritage teach us about Jews in the armed forces?

Our Heritage of Peace and War

The Jewish greeting, *shalom* (peace), reflects the basic wish that all people have: to live peaceably with their neighbors. The fact that throughout our Jewish history so many of our heroes have been military leaders shows how difficult it is for people to live in peace. Abraham, Gideon, Saul, David, Judah Maccabee, and Bar Kohbah, are some of the well-known figures who have led the Jewish nation in battle. Yet, the Torah reminds us, we must always try to avoid war by first offering peace to those who would be our enemies. (Deuteronomy 20:10)

Jewish Law and Military Service

Since the time of the exile from the Holy Land, Jews have served in the armed forces of non-Jewish countries. What happens if the requirements of military service conflict with Jewish law? For example, how can a Jew keep kosher while serving in a non-Jewish army? During the revolutionary war, an observant Jew and Patriot named Reuben Etting faced this problem. He enlisted in the Maryland militia and was captured by the British. While a prisoner of war, he refused to eat pork, which was the main food offered to him. He suffered from malnutrition, became sick with tuberculosis, and died from the effects of his imprisonment.

Today, The United States Armed Forces provides kosher food for Jewish soldiers. But what about a prisoner of war, or a soldier in combat who has finished his kosher rations? Suppose a fellow soldier offers him non-kosher food. The rabbis have ruled that under circumstances such as these, a Jewish soldier may eat forbidden food.

A biblical scene, by the nineteenth-century artist Gustave Doré, showing soldiers in King David's army.

Shabbat and Holy Days

May a Jewish soldier fight on the Sabbath or a holy day? If at all possible, this should be avoided. In 1776, Hart Jacobs of New York asked to be excused from military duty on Friday night because it was part of the Jewish Sabbath. The Committee of Safety, the rebel authority in New York during the revolutionary war, ordered "that he be exempted from military on that night of the week," and that he perform "his full tour of duty on other nights."

As a general rule, the Sabbath and holy days may be violated to save a life. If there has been an attack on those days, a Jewish soldier may fight to defend his country. This is what happened on Yom Kippur, 1973, when thousands of Israeli soldiers found themselves going to war.

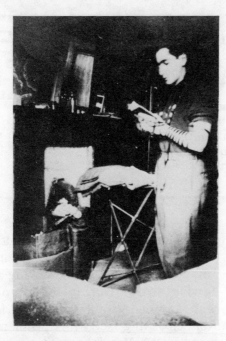

Yom Kippur in the Army

The commands of our faith can be combined with the demands of military life. Even wounded soldiers can gather together and pray as Jews. This report, from a Jewish newspaper of 1862, records the experience of Colonel Grun, an officer in the Civil War, when he found himself spending Yom Kippur in a military hospital:

> Being slightly wounded, he was taken to the hospital. . . . Having found ten coreligionists in the hospital, the colonel resolved at once to offer up prayers. . . . Amidst the thunder of the cannon, these wounded soldiers began to recite the prayer of *Neilah* [the last of the five Yom Kippur services], the colonel officiating. . . . Since the time of the Maccabees there was not celebrated a Day of Atonement in so splendid a manner. [*American Jewish Archives*, 1961]

Top: On leave in Belgium, in 1945, a Jewish soldier dons tefilin for morning prayers.

Middle: Holiday services for American soldiers stationed in Australia, 1942.

Bottom: Jewish crew members of the U.S.S. Missouri celebrate Pesaḥ near Okinawa, 1945.

Left: Commodore Uriah Philips Levy, commander of the Mediterranean Fleet, fought to abolish corporal punishment in the United States Navy. Center: Frederick Knefler joined the Union army as a private. By the end of the Civil War he was a general. Right: Private Isidor Cohen, who lost a leg in the Spanish-American War of 1898, is one of hundreds of thousands of Jews who have served in the armed forces of the United States.

Left: Sergeant Benjamin Kaufman won the Congressional Medal of Honor for bravery during World War I. Center: Lieutenant Colonel Jack Jacobs won the Congressional Medal of Honor for saving the lives of at least 13 soldiers in Vietnam. Right: Vice Admiral Hyman G. Rickover, known as the "father of the atomic-powered submarine."

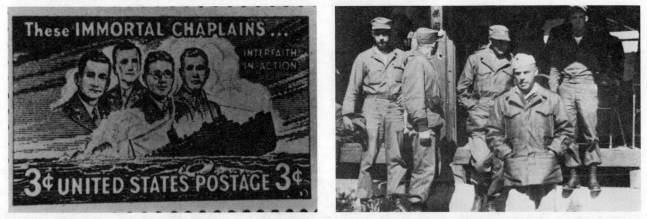

Left: This postage stamp honors four chaplains who died when the U.S.S. Dorchester went down in 1942. One of the chaplains was (far right) Rabbi Alexander Goode. Right: Colonel Howard S. Levie (front), a member of the staff of the United Nations Command Korean Armistice Delegation, was author of the peace agreement that ended the Korean War.

CLOSE-UPS: *Jews on the Frontier*

Receipt for land warrants given by Daniel Boone to the firm of Cohen & Isaacs.

KENTUCKY

In 1781, the Richmond firm of Cohen and Isaacs hired Daniel Boone to survey land in Kentucky. The Gratz brothers and Joseph Simon also owned much land in Kentucky and sponsored expeditions to establish settlements there. Michael Gratz's son Benjamin came to Lexington in 1819. He supported the city's educational institutions and helped organize the Lexington and Ohio Railroad.

In 1834, citizens of Louisville petitioned the Kentucky House of Representatives for permission to establish an "Israelitish Congregation" there. Two years later, the first congregation was formally organized.

Benjamin Gratz

VIRGINIA

There were a few Jewish pioneers in colonial Virginia. In 1764, Michael Israel bought 80 acres of land in western Virginia. The number of Jewish settlers greatly increased after 1785, when the state legislature passed

Thomas Jefferson's bill guaranteeing religious freedom. In 1789, Congregation Beth Shalome was founded in Richmond. Its members included Jacob I. Cohen and Jacob Mordecai.

Gustavus A. Myers (1801–1869) served on the city council of Richmond, Virginia for almost thirty years.

MICHIGAN

The first Jews in Michigan came to trade with the Indians. Ezekiel Solomon opened a trading post at Fort Michilimackinac in 1761, when the area was still part of British Canada. Solomon was captured by Indians during the 1763 massacre at the fort, but was later freed for a ransom.

Chapman Abraham settled in Fort Detroit in 1762. A year later, he was canoeing up the Detroit River when he was captured by Chippewa Indians. They tortured him and stole his merchandise, but he was finally able to escape.

The Jewish presence in Michigan grew during the German-Jewish migration of the 1840s. German Jews settled in Ann Arbor, where they first held services in 1845 and purchased land for a cemetery around 1848. Jews also settled in Jackson, Kalamazoo, Grand Rapids, Lansing, and Detroit. Temple Beth El, the oldest congregation in Detroit, was founded in 1850.

An eighteenth-century drawing of a fur trader and an Indian.

John Jacob Hays traded furs with the Indians and was also a farmer in Cahokia, Illinois. In 1798, he was appointed Cahokia's sheriff. For the next twenty years, this log cabin served as his courthouse.

ILLINOIS

The Gratz brothers, David Franks, and Joseph Simon were partners in Illinois land speculation in the eighteenth century. There were also isolated Jewish settlers such as Sheriff John Jacob Hays of Cahokia.

In 1846, the first congregation in Chicago was founded by fifteen Jews. It was called Kehillath Anshe Ma'arav, "Congregation of the People of the West." By 1860, there were about fifteen hundred Jews in the city.

Solomon Heydenfeldt practiced law and served as a judge of the Tallapoosa, Alabama county court. He later moved to California, where he was elected a judge of the Supreme Court.

ALABAMA

Although Abram Mordecai had settled in Alabama by 1785, it was not until 1820 that a Jewish community was founded there, in the city of Mobile. In 1841, grounds were set aside for a cemetery and three years later, Congregation Sharai Shomayim u-Maskil Dol was founded. By the Civil War, there were also Jewish communities in Montgomery (1849) and Huntsville (1860).

When Abraham Jonas arrived in Quincy, Illinois, in 1838, he met Abraham Lincoln. The two became lifelong friends and political allies.

Simon and Melanie, children of John and Jannette Mayer.

Joseph Jonas

MISSISSIPPI

Some historians believe that Jewish services were held in Natchez, Mississippi as early as 1798. There were Jewish cemeteries in that city and in Biloxi by the 1830s, but it was not until 1840 that the first congregation, B'nai Israel of Natchez, was officially established. Services were held in private homes or rented quarters until 1867, when a building was purchased for use as a synagogue.

Most of the Jews in the state were peddlers or storekeepers. John Mayer had a shoe store in Natchez. He and his wife Jannette were leaders of the city's Jewish community. In the 1860s, he was head of the *ḥevrah kadisha* (the burial society).

OHIO

When Joseph Jonas arrived in Cincinnati in 1817, many of its citizens had never seen a Jew. "Is thee truly a Jew?" one woman asked. After examining him, she said, "Why thee is no different than any other man!"

Congregation Bene Israel was organized in Cincinnati in 1824. In 1839, the Israelite Society was founded in Cleveland. For much of the nineteenth century, Cincinnati was one of the most important cities in American Jewish life. This was largely due to the leadership of Rabbi Isaac Mayer Wise, who made the city a center of Reform Jewish life. The Hebrew Union College, a rabbinical school for the Reform movement, was founded there in 1875.

In the 1830s and 1840s, a large number of Ashkenazic Jews immigrated to the United States. Many of these newcomers became peddlers, settling in all parts of the country. A. Heidenreich of Riga, Russia, opened this store in McComb, Mississippi.

The first building of Hebrew Union College, in Cincinatti.

Castro County and the town of Castroville are named after the French Jew, Henri Castro, who sponsored settlers in west Texas.

The Philipson house in St. Genevieve, Missouri.

TEXAS

There is no way of knowing how many people in southwestern states today are descended from the Marranos who fled there to escape the Inquisition. Some scholars estimate that there are thousands.

One of the first identifiable Jews in Texas was Samuel Izaacs, who arrived in 1821. About two hundred Jews fought in the battles for Texan independence from Mexico, including Dr. Moses Albert Levy, who organized a group of sixty-six men from New Orleans to fight in Texas. In 1835, Levy and his men were among those who successfully attacked the Alamo, a mission and fortress in San Antonio.

Jacob de Cordova helped found the first Jewish house of worship in Houston in 1850. Galveston's B'nai Israel was founded in 1868, followed by congregations in Brownsville (1870) and Dallas (1871).

MISSOURI

In 1803, the United States bought the Louisiana Territory, a huge chunk of land, from the French. Jews could now enter the area west of the Mississippi, from which the French had previously tried to bar them. Jacob Philipson came to St. Louis in 1807 and opened a store. Only thirty years later were there finally ten Jews to form a *minyan* (the minimum number of Jews required for prayer services) for the High Holy Days. Three years later, the community purchased land for a cemetery. In 1855, Congregation B'nai El began construction of the first synagogue in the Mississippi Valley. Congregations were also established in St. Joseph (1860) and Kansas City (1870).

German-born Adolphus Sterne had a trading post in Nacogdoches, Texas. A well-educated man, Sterne spoke Yiddish, French, German, Spanish, and several Indian languages. He liked to amuse his friends by pretending to be an auctioneer and conducting the bidding in Yiddish or Choctaw.

The B'nai El Synagogue, on the southeast corner of Sixth and Cerre Streets, St. Louis.

LOUISIANA

Louisiana was settled by the French. Article I of the *Code Noir* (Black Code) of the colony, issued in 1724, provided that "the Jews, who may have been established there, be expelled from the Colony within three months under the penalty of confiscation of body and property." Article III prohibited "the exercise of any other religion than Catholic." Although the French government tried to bar Jews from the colony, there is evidence that there were some Jews in Louisiana in the middle of the eighteenth century. Among them was a Dutch-born merchant, Isaac Rodriguez Monsanto, whose agents traveled throughout the colony trading at villages and military posts.

Notable nineteenth century Jewish residents included the charitable Judah Touro; Louisiana's senator and later Secretary of State of the Confederacy, Judah Benjamin; and Henry M. Hymans, the state's lieutenant-governor. The artist Theodore Sydney Moïse, who traveled throughout the South painting portraits of plantation owners and their families, made his home in New Orleans.

An 1843 portrait of the American politician, Henry Clay, by Theodore Sydney Moise.

Gershom Kursheedt, a businessman in New Orleans and leader of its Jewish community in the 1840s.

III · THE CIVIL WAR

וּמִלְחָמָה הָיְתָה בֵין־רְחַבְעָם וּבֵין יָרָבְעָם כָּל־הַיָּמִים.

"And there was war between Rehoboam and Jeroboam continually."
I Kings 14:30

Almost every nation has fought a civil war at some time in its history. Even the ancient Israelites fought each other. The Bible tells us that after the death of King Solomon, the tribes in the south accepted his son, Rehoboam, as their king. But the northern tribes rebelled and made another man, Jeroboam, their ruler. What had been one nation split into two: Israel in the north and Judah in the south. (I Kings 12—14)

America's civil war took place between 1861 and 1865. One of its major causes was the dispute over slavery. There were about one hundred fifty

Above: The Civil War battle at Perryville, Kentucky (1862), sketched by Henry Mosler.

thousand Jews in the country during the Civil War, and they were just as divided as the rest of the nation. They tended to have the same attitudes as their non-Jewish neighbors. Jews in the South supported the Confederacy and Jews in the North, the Union.

Preparations for Defense at Cincinnati—Citizens in the Trenches, *sketched by Henry Mosler.*

CHAPTER ONE
THE JEWS OF THE NORTH

Anti-Slavery Immigrants

Before 1750, many of America's Jews were Sephardim. They had come from Spain, Portugal, England, and Holland and had settled in the old, established Jewish communities of both the northern and southern United States.

By the middle of the nineteenth century, a new wave of immigration brought many more Ashkenazim to America. There had been Ashkenazim among the earliest immigrants of colonial times, but they began arriving in greater numbers after 1836, to escape famine and anti-Semitism. In 1848, a series of revolutions swept across Europe, and many Jews participated with hopes of gaining political equality for their people. But the revolutions failed, and many of these Jews came to America.

Because they had recently fought for their own freedom in Europe, many of these immigrants sympathized with the plight of the black slaves. Some of them were active in the anti-slavery abolitionist movement. Others joined the thousands of Jews who fought in the Union army.

German-born Moritz Pinner went to Kansas City in 1856. He established and edited the Kansas Post, which he used to promote the abolitionist cause. Pinner hoped to make Kansas a free state. Pro-slavery factions threatened his life and tried unsuccessfully to make him leave the area. Pinner later became active in politics and was a delegate to the 1860 Republican convention that nominated Lincoln for the presidency.

Ernestine Potovsky Rose, a feminist and abolitionist, was born in Poland. She was the daughter of an orthodox rabbi. Rose disputed the widely-held idea that slaves' lives were "happy and carefree." "Even if slaveholders treated their slaves with the utmost kindness and charity," she wrote, "it is none the less slavery; for what does slavery mean? . . . . Slavery is, not to belong to yourself—to be robbed of yourself."

Isidor Bush lived in the slave state of Missouri, but was an abolitionist who believed in the preservation of the Union. He argued that slavery "destroyed God's noblest work—a free people." Elected to Missouri's constitutional conventions, he urged that the slaves be freed. Bush was a founder of the first synagogue in St. Louis and was publisher of the German-Jewish weekly, Israel's Herold.

No Jewish Chaplains

Between seven and ten thousand Jewish soldiers served in the armies of North and South. When these men got sick or wounded, or when they wanted to observe the Jewish holidays, they wanted rabbis. But no rabbis could be found in the Union army. Congress had passed a law in July 1861, declaring that all military chaplains had to belong to "some Christian group."

This law ignored the First Amendment to the Constitution, which says that "Congress shall make no law respecting an establishment of religion." Now Congress was saying that only Christians could serve as chaplains. Wasn't this law an attempt to establish Christianity as the official religion of the army? Not only did the law prevent rabbis from becoming chaplains, it was also a threat to the religious freedom of all Jews.

A portrait of President Abraham Lincoln by the Sephardic artist, Solomon Nunes Carvalho, of Charleston, South Carolina.

Arnold Fischel led the fight to have Jewish chaplains serve in the Union army.

The Jews Protest

The Jews began a long campaign to change this law, headed by a man named Arnold Fischel. He had been chosen as chaplain by the soldiers of Cameron's Dragoons, a Pennsylvania regiment that included a large number of Jews. But when Fischel applied for the position, the army told him that it would accept no Jew as a military chaplain.

There were newspaper editorials, sermons, and petitions about the problem. Fischel even met with President Lincoln, who proposed "a new law broad enough to cover what is desired by you in behalf of the Israelites." Finally, in July 1862, Congress passed a new law stating that chaplains had to be ministers of some religious denomination. This wording was broad enough to include Jews as well as Christians. Two months later, Jacob Frankel became the first Jewish chaplain in the United States military. The first Jewish chaplain in combat was Ferdinand Sarner, who was at the battles of Chancellorville and Gettysburg.

Grant's Expulsion Order

Shortly after the chaplaincy problem was solved, a second event shocked Union Jews into action. In December 1862, General Ulysses S. Grant issued an order expelling all Jews from Kentucky and Tennessee. Grant accused the Jews of trading with the enemy, the South. He said that they were taking advantage of the war by making money on goods in tight supply. Although he did not present any evidence to prove his charge, the general forced every Jew—women, babies, even veterans of the Union army—to leave the area. When they asked why they had to go, they were told: "Because you are Jews, and are neither a benefit to the Union or Confederacy."

A portrait of General Ulysses S. Grant by Albert Rosenthal of Philadelphia.

A sketch made in 1862 by Henry Mosler, showing Union troops stationed in Kentucky.

The order saddened and infuriated Jews throughout the North. Jewish men were fighting and dying for the Union cause. Jewish women were nursing the wounded, caring for widows and orphans, and raising money for the war effort. How could their country repay them with such an order? It was a frightening reminder of the persecution that many of them had recently left behind them in Europe.

Leopold Karpeles, who came to America from Prague, served in the Union army. He was awarded a Medal of Honor because he "rallied the retreating troops" at the Battle of the Wilderness in 1864 and "induced them to check the advance of the enemy." The Civil War Medal of Honor also was awarded to several other Jews, including Abraham Cohn, Benjamin Levy, and David Orbanski.

At charitable events such as this Purim ball, money was raised to buy clothing, medicine, food, and other supplies for the relief of Civil War widows, orphans, and wounded soldiers.

A Plea to Lincoln

Both Jews and non-Jews protested that the order was unfair. Cesar J. Kaskel, a Jew from Kentucky, went to Washington to make a personal plea to the President. He had been expelled from his home because of Grant's order and he begged Lincoln to overturn it. The President was shocked by Kaskel's story. It was one thing, he said, to expel traitors and profiteers. It was quite another thing to throw out an entire group of people, loyal supporters and defenders of the Union. Upon Lincoln's direct command, Grant's order was revoked.

Abraham Lincoln was a good friend to the Jewish people. When he was killed, thousands of Jews marched in the parades that honored his memory.

Left: Joseph Seligman's banking firm in New York helped sell more than $200 million in Union bonds, to support the Union's war effort. Right: Cesar J. Kaskel went to Washington, D.C. to ask President Lincoln to revoke General Grant's expulsion order.

CLOSE-UPS: *Yankee Jews*

A PASSOVER SEDER IN THE UNION ARMY

Joseph A. Joel was a Jewish soldier in the Union army. He later described an 1862 Passover celebration that took place on a West Virginia battlefield:

> The ceremonies were passing off very nicely, until we arrived at the part where the bitter herb was to be taken. . . . The herb was very bitter and very fiery like Cayenne pepper, and excited our thirst to such a degree, that we forgot the law authorizing us to drink only four cups, and the consequence was we drank up all the cider. Those that drank the more freely became excited, and one thought he was Moses,

another Aaron, and one had the audacity to call himself a Pharaoh. The consequence was a skirmish, with nobody hurt, only Moses, Aaron and Pharaoh, had to be carried to the camp. . . . There, in the wild woods of West Virginia, away from home and friends, we consecrated and offered up to the ever-loving God of Israel our prayers and sacrifice. I doubt whether the spirits of our forefathers, had they been looking down on us, standing there with our arms by our side ready for an attack, faithful to our God and our cause, would have imagined themselves amongst mortals, enacting this commemoration of the scene that transpired in Egypt.
> [*Jewish Messenger*, March 30, 1866]

A modern drawing of the Union Army seder attended by Joseph A. Joel.

Julius and Bertha Ochs and their children.

A YANKEE OFFICER AND HIS REBEL WIFE

Bertha Levy, an immigrant from Germany, was raised in Natchez, Mississippi, where she became devoted to the Southern cause. But her husband, German-born Julius Ochs, was sympathetic to the North.

Shocked by the way the slaves were treated in the South, he once wrote in his diary:

Beatings and lashings with ugly thongs were frequent occurrences. These sights sickened me. Once I saw a poor wretch so horribly beaten that tears of pity gushed from my eyes. [Sulzberger and Dryfoos, *Iphigene: Memoirs of Iphigene Ochs Sulzberger*]

In 1861, the Ochs family was living in Cincinnati. Julius enlisted in the Union army and was soon appointed a captain. His unit was ordered to prevent the smuggling of arms and supplies from Cincinnati in the North to Kentucky in the South.

One day, Bertha put her infant son into his carriage and started to walk across the Ohio River Bridge to Kentucky. She was stopped, the carriage was searched, and she was discovered trying to smuggle medicine to the Confederates. Only the fact that she was the wife of a loyal Union officer saved her from arrest.

At Bertha's funeral, her coffin was draped in a Confederate flag. Julius was later buried next to her, his coffin covered by the Stars and Stripes.

A JEWISH ABOLITIONIST RIDES WITH JOHN BROWN

August (Anshel) Bondi, an immigrant from Vienna, was a fierce opponent of slavery. His feelings were so strong that he joined the forces of John Brown, the famed abolitionist, and fought to keep Kansas from becoming a slave state. Two other Jews were in the band, Theodor Weiner and Jacob Benjamin. They

often talked things over in Yiddish, even, as Bondi later reported, in the middle of battle:

I called out to him. *'Nu, was meinen sie yetzt?'* [Well, what do you think of it now?] His answer, *'Was soll ich meinen?'* [What should I think?] *'Sof odom muves.'* [The end of man is death.] In spite of the whistling bullets, I laughed when he said, *'Machen wir dem alten mann sonst broges.'* [Look out, or we'll make the old man angry.] [August Bondi, *Autobiography*]

The "old man" they referred to was John Brown.

In 1861 Bondi enlisted in the Union army because "as a *Jehudi* [Jew] I had the duty to perform, to defend the institutions which gave equal rights to all beliefs." Bondi once described himself as "Never orthodox, but a consistent Jew nevertheless. I believed in the continuance and upholding of all the ceremonial laws."

August Bondi

CIVIL WAR ARTISTS

In Civil War days, cameras were still a new invention. Because there were few photographers, the armies often hired artists to travel with them and make illustrated records of the war.

Among the Civil War artists with the Union army was a Jew named Henry Mosler. He was attached to the staff of General R. W. Johnson and also covered the war for *Harper's Weekly*. After the war, he studied art in Cincinnati, Paris, and Dusseldorf. His work includes scenes from American history, such as the painting of Betsy Ross and her friends sewing the first American flag, and another of George Washington crossing the Delaware.

Another Civil War artist, Max Rosenthal, followed the Army of the Potomac as its official illustrator. He produced color plates for a medical and surgical history of the war. Rosenthal studied art in Paris and at the Pennsylvania Academy of Fine Arts. After the war, he worked with his son Albert.

Samples of works by these and other Jewish artists appear throughout this book.

Henry Mosler at work.

The sculptor Moses Jacob Ezekiel was raised in Virginia and served with the Confederate army. He was chosen to design the Confederate Monument at Arlington National Cemetery, which honors those who died in the Civil War and symbolizes a reunited nation. Around its base is a biblical verse from Isaiah 2:4, expressing the statue's theme of peace: "And they shall beat their swords into plowshares and their spears into pruning hooks."

Proclamation of Emancipation by Max Rosenthal celebrated Abraham Lincoln and the freeing of the slaves.

FROM OUR JEWISH HERITAGE: Slavery

*Many Jews supported the movement to abolish slavery.
What is there about the Jewish heritage that might make
Jews especially sensitive to the evils of slavery?*

The Pesaḥ Seder

Each year, millions of Jews recline at their tables and celebrate the holiday of *Pesaḥ*, or Passover. At a special dinner, the *seder*, we tell the story of the Hebrews who were slaves in Egypt: how they cried out to God, how God answered their prayers, took them out of Egypt, and made them a free people.

At the seder, we eat *maror*, bitter herbs, which symbolizes the bitter life our ancestors led in Egypt. We also eat *ḥaroset*, a mixture of fruits, nuts, spices, and wine, which represents the materials that the Hebrew slaves used to make bricks. Ḥaroset reminds us of the hard physical labor that was required of the slaves.

During the eight days of Pesaḥ, we also eat matzah, unleavened bread. Matzah is also called *laḥma anya*, "the bread of affliction." It is the food of the poor. Matzah reminds us what it is like to be oppressed and hungry.

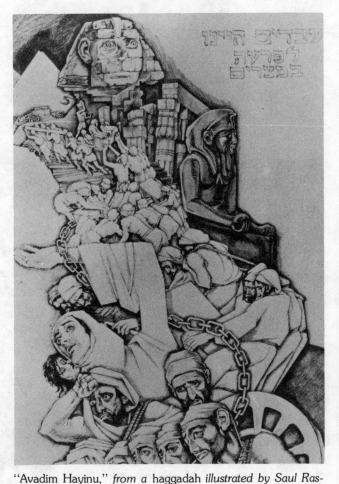

"*Avadim Hayinu,*" *from a* haggadah *illustrated by Saul Raskin.*

The Meaning of Pesaḥ

"*Avadim hayinu l'faro b'mitzrayim,*" Jews recite. "We were slaves unto pharaoh in Egypt." Note that we do not say, "our ancestors were slaves," but "*we* were slaves." The word "we" reminds every one of us that if God had not taken the Hebrews out of bondage in Egypt, we might still be slaves.

Israel as the Servant of God

What does the Bible mean when it refers to people as slaves? The Hebrew word *eved*, which is translated as "servant" or "slave," is from the root *avad*, meaning to work, to labor, or to serve. The word usually refers to someone who is dependent on someone in a position of authority. For example, the king's ministers are called *avdai ha-me-lekh*, "servants of the king." Even the prophets are referred to as God's servants.

Most importantly, the people of Israel are referred to as the servants of God. "For to me the people of Israel are servants, they are my servants whom I brought forth out of the land of Egypt." (Leviticus 25:55) It is this relationship between God and Israel that forms the model for the relationship between master and slave. Just as God treats His servant Israel with compassion and mercy, so a master must treat his slaves. As our sages teach us, all are equal before God, "women, slaves, poor and rich."

Jews and Oppressed Peoples

Perhaps it is because of their remembered experience of slavery that Jews have always been unusually sensitive to the cries of oppressed peoples. Throughout their history, Jews have responded out of proportion to their numbers as leaders of causes such as the trade union movement to better the condition of workers, and the civil rights movement seeking equality for black Americans. Having been oppressed themselves, Jews have learned to cherish freedom.

Jews and blacks marching together at a civil rights rally in the 1960s.

A detail from Proclamation of Emancipation *by Max Rosenthal, showing the whipping of a slave. When the laws relating to the treatment of slaves were given at Sinai, the Israelites were told, "You shall remember that you were a servant in the land of Egypt." (Deuteronomy 5:15) This meant: do not forget what it is like to be a slave; put yourself in the slave's place; treat the slave as you would have wished to be treated in Egypt.*

CHAPTER TWO
THE JEWS OF THE SOUTH

Confederate Loyalists

The Jews of the South were mostly American-born members of families that had long been established in the region. Most of them fought for the Confederacy and supported slavery. In the South at that time, slavery was considered a normal part of life; the Jews tended to feel the same as the rest of the white population. An 1860 census showed that about 25 percent of white Southern adults owned slaves. The percentage among Jews probably was about the same.

Some of the more prosperous Jews owned plantations. Raphael Moses of Columbus, Georgia, had forty-seven slaves. Nathan Nathans, the president of Beth Elohim Congregation in Charleston, farmed a large plantation on the Cooper River. There were even a few Jewish slave traders.

An 1859 advertisement by a Jewish slave trader in Lumpkin, Georgia.

Raphael Moses of Georgia was a fifth-generation Sephardi-American. He and his three sons enlisted in the Confederate army, where he rose to the rank of major. Moses was proud of his Jewish heritage and once ran for Congress because he "wanted to go to Congress as a Jew."

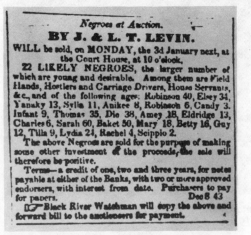

An advertisement for the sale of slaves by Jacob Levin and his partner. Levin was not hated by his fellow Jews because he traded slaves. On the contrary, he was acting rabbi and head of the Jewish community of Columbia, South Carolina.

Assimilation

In the South, whites regarded slaves as property rather than as human beings. One would think that because of the Jews' religious heritage, they would have been inspired to treat slaves more humanely. But many Jews in the South had intermarried or assimilated and were lost to their people and their faith.

By 1840, for example, the Jews of New Orleans had become so assimilated that an observer found only two homes where Shabbat was observed. "Two-thirds of the Jews did not have their sons circumcised," the observer wrote, and "not even fifty of the Jewish boys could read Hebrew."

Few Jews retained their ties to Judaism. But even those who did so were full participants in Southern society. Most treated their slaves no differently than did other slave-owners. There were Jews who helped capture runaway slaves, testified against them in court, and saw to it that they were punished. Most Southern Jews did not think about slavery in terms of the humane teachings of their religion.

Acceptance of Jews

The South had its share of anti-Semitism, but the Jews there had reached higher levels of social and political acceptance than had Jews in the North. In the South the most important social distinction was not between Jews and Christians, but between blacks and whites.

Top: In the 1840s, Judah Touro of New Orleans gave the money to buy an old church and convert it into a synagogue. Touro was the son of the ḥazan of Newport's Synagogue, Isaac Touro. Middle: Detail from Max Rosenthal's Proclamation of Emancipation, *showing a black woman and her child being sold at a southern slave auction. Bottom: Jacob de Cordova, Texas real-estate developer, editor, and politician, said that he wanted it to be "understood that our feelings and education have always been pro-slavery." De Cordova, a Texas state representative and senator, was one of a number of Jews who held political office in the pre-war South.*

Anti-Semitism Grows

In hard times, Jews often become scapegoats for other people's troubles. And since the Civil War caused much suffering in both North and South, Jews often found themselves the object of growing resentment. In the North, for example, economic tensions had led to General Grant's order expelling all the Jews from Kentucky. Similar tensions existed in the South.

As the South began to lose the war, many Southerners began to blame Jews for their misfortunes. They blamed Jewish merchants and storekeepers for high prices and supply shortages. Newspaper articles attacked Jewish "exploiters" and "speculators." In one Georgia town, a group of armed Christian women looted Jewish stores. The women claimed that the Jews were making fortunes from the war while their husbands were out fighting it. This was an outrageous charge because thousands of Jewish men were in the Southern army. The Jews had become scapegoats for the South's defeat.

Edwin Warren Moise of South Carolina gave his entire fortune of $10,000 to pay for a company of cavalrymen that became part of the Confederate army. He fought in northern Virginia, was wounded in Gettysburg, and was promoted to the rank of major.

The Civil War divided some Jewish families, pitting brothers against brothers, fathers against sons. Abraham Jonas, an Illinois politician and a close friend of President Lincoln's, had five sons. One of them, Edward, was an officer in an Illinois regiment. Another brother, Major Charles H. Jonas (right), fought for the Confederacy and was captured by Union troops. Lincoln gave permission for Jonas to be released so that he could visit his dying father.

American Jews Reunited

The emotional ties that bind Jews together were strained, but not broken, by the Civil War. At the close of the war, an editorial in the *New York Jewish Record* noted that "fraternal blood has been spilled by violent hands." The newspaper added that "the hand of the Southern Israelite has been found raised against his Northern brother."

After the war, the once proud and wealthy Jewish communities of the South appealed to their fellow Jews in the North for help. Northern Jews responded at once. In 1865, for example, the communities of New York and Philadelphia sent five thousand pounds of matzah to Savannah, so the Jews there could celebrate Passover.

When Union forces captured the Mississippi town of Natchez, a local Jewish family, the Mayers, invited two Jewish soldiers into their home. As one of the family members, Clara, later wrote: "Many were the heated discussions between these Yankees and our rebel family until Mother forbade political wrangling, but encouraged social affinity." Mrs. Mayer encouraged so much togetherness that two of her daughters ended up marrying the two Northern men. With these and similar acts of kindness, forgiveness, and generosity, America's Jews began to heal the wounds of war.

CLOSE-UPS: *Confederate Jews*

"THE BRAINS OF THE CONFEDERACY"

The Jew who had the greatest political power during the Civil War was Judah Philip Benjamin. He was born in the Virgin Islands to a Sephardic family that moved to Charleston when he was a boy. He studied law in New Orleans and owned a plantation with one hundred forty slaves.

In 1852, Benjamin was elected U.S. Senator from Louisiana. He made brilliant speeches in the Senate in support of slavery and the constitutional right of the southern states to leave the Union. In 1861, Louisiana seceded, and Benjamin resigned from the Senate.

Jefferson Davis, President of the Confederacy, appointed Benjamin its Attorney General. Often called "the brains of the Confederacy," Benjamin later served as the South's Secretary of War and Secretary of State.

Although Benjamin never denied that he was a Jew, he married a non-Jew and had no formal ties with Judaism. Even so, his enemies would not let him forget that he was Jewish. "A grander rascal than this Jew Benjamin does not exist in the Confederacy," one Confederate general said about him. Benjamin was also known as "Mr. Davis' pet Jew" because Davis rarely made a decision without consulting him.

After the South's defeat, Benjamin escaped to Florida disguised as a woman. He took a small boat to Cuba and from there went to England, where he had a successful career as a lawyer.

Judah Philip Benjamin

The ruins of Benjamin's plantation at Bellechasse, near New Orleans.

Lazarus and Sara Straus

STOREKEEPERS IN GEORGIA

Lazarus and Sara Straus owned a store in Talbotton, Georgia. Although they owned slaves, the Strauses obeyed the Torah's command to "remember that you were a servant in the land of Egypt." They treated their slaves well. Lazarus taught each male slave a trade; one was a shoemaker and another was a tailor. Their son Oscar recalled, "If we children spoke to the slaves harshly or disregarded their feelings, we were promptly checked and reprimanded by our parents."

During the Civil War, supplies were scarce and prices climbed. A grand jury in Talbotton decided that the high prices were the fault of Jewish merchants and condemned them for their "evil and unpatriotic conduct." As the only Jews in Talbotton, the Strauses were very upset by this and moved to another town in Georgia.

After the war, the Strauses settled in New York, where their sons Nathan and Isidor became owners of Macy's department store. Oscar, a lawyer, was appointed Secretary of Commerce and Labor by Theodore Roosevelt. He was the first Jew be a member of a United States Cabinet.

such talk could be considered treason. The women were suspected of spying for the Confederacy. Philip was placed under house arrest, and his wife and daughters were held in the attic of another house. A month later, the family was forced to leave the capital.

Not long after their arrival in New Orleans, the city was captured by Union forces. The Union commander described Eugenia as "an uncommon bad and dangerous woman, stirring up strife and inciting to riot." He accused her, among other things, of laughing at the sight of a Yankee's funeral. Eugenia was sent to a prison on an island in the Gulf of Mexico.

She was released three months later, but never stopped defending the Confederacy. When the South lost the war, Eugenia said sadly that "God, in His wisdom, decided against us."

Eugenia Levy Phillips

Philip Phillips

A CONFEDERATE SPY?

Philip Phillips was a lawyer and a former congressman from Alabama. He was loyal to the South, but he did not think that the Southern states should leave the Union. But because his wife and daughters were so passionately devoted to the South, the whole family got in trouble.

In 1861, just before the war began, the Phillips family was living in Washington, D.C. Eugenia and her daughters talked openly about their belief that the Southern states should secede. Philip later complained that he could not make his wife and daughters see that

A SOUTHERN WOMAN COMPLAINS

Eleanor H. Cohen was a young Jewish woman from South Carolina who was loyal to the Confederate cause. In 1865, when it was clear that the South had lost the war, she wrote in her diary:

Our servants, born and reared in our hands, hitherto devoted to us, freed by Lincoln, left us today. It is a severe trial to mother, and quite a loss to me. . . . This is one of the fruits of war. I, who believe in the institution of slavery, regret deeply its being

abolished. I am accustomed to have them wait on me, and I dislike white servants very much. . . .
The Fourth [of July] was celebrated by the "freed-man" [the freed slaves]. They had orations, a bar-becue, fireworks, and a general jubilee. To me it was a sad day of humiliation. . . . Our cause is lost; we are conquered and feel the yoke. [Jacob R. Marcus, *Memoirs of American Jews*]

JUDAISM IN THE CONFEDERATE ARMY

Some Confederate Jewish soldiers struggled to keep their religious identity. Private Isaac Gleitzman of Arkansas received the Confederate Cross of Honor "for conspicuous gallantry in the field." He was equally proud that during his four years of military service, he never ate non-kosher food. He carried two mess kits into battle: one for milk and one for meat.

In 1861, Rabbi M. J. Michelbacher asked General Robert E. Lee to grant leave to all Jewish soldiers serving in Virginia, so that they could come to Rosh Hashanah services at his Richmond synagogue. Lee replied that war conditions prevented him from giving permission to everyone, because it might "jeopardize a cause you have so much at heart. . . ." However, he did permit individual Jews to apply for leave.

Apparently, conditions had changed by 1862. Private Lewis Leon, a sharpshooter in a North Carolina regiment, wrote in his diary:

Sept. 19—This morning they read an order from our father R. E. Lee in which he gave furlough into Richmond of all Israelites in honor of the Jewish New Year. Wortheim, Oppenheim, Norment, Katz and myself, as well as Lt. E. Cohen, worshipped. [Lewis Leon, *Diary of a Tar Heel Confederate Soldier*]

Eleanor H. Cohen

General Lee's letter to Rabbi Michelbacher.

General Robert E. Lee, by the sculptor Moses Jacob Ezekiel.

A DEBATE ON SLAVERY
The Views of Ten Jewish Leaders

MORRIS JACOB RAPHALL

In 1861, Morris Jacob Raphall, rabbi at B'nai Jeshurun synagogue in New York, gave a sermon entitled, "The Bible View of Slavery." He pointed out that the Bible does not regard slaveholding as a sin, and some of its greatest heroes, such as Abraham, Isaac, and Jacob, were slaveholders. Raphall said he was "no friend to slavery," but could not twist the words of the Bible.

Raphall stressed a major difference between the biblical view of slavery and the southern view. In the Bible, he said, the slave was "a *person* in whom the dignity of human nature is to be respected; he has rights." In the South, he said, the slave is "a *thing*, and a thing can have no rights."

Raphall had been asked to give his sermon by the American Society for Promoting National Unity, a group of Jews and Christians from both the North and South. Like Raphall, they were opposed to slavery but would tolerate it in order to save the Union. Among the other rabbis who supported the Society were George Jacobs of Richmond, James Gutheim of New Orleans, and J. Blumenthal of Montgomery, Alabama, all southerners. During the Civil War, all of them supported the Confederacy. The issue for them was not belief in slavery, but loyalty to the area in which they lived.

Morris Jacob Raphall

DAVID EINHORN

One of the people who attacked Raphall's sermon most bitterly was David Einhorn, leader of Har Sinai Temple in Baltimore. He was ashamed that what he called a "pro-slavery" sermon had been given by a Jew, "a descendant of the race that offers daily praises to God for deliverance out of the house of bondage in Egypt, and even to-day suffers under the yoke of slavery in most places of the old world. . . ."

Einhorn argued that the Bible merely tolerated slavery as something that eventually should be abolished. He admitted that great men such as Jacob owned slaves. But Jacob also had more than one wife at a time, a practice which the rabbis later decided was improper. Einhorn's point was that Jewish law may change because of new interpretations or new conditions. He wanted Jews to condemn slavery, even though the Bible never did so. He was concerned not only with the words of the Bible but with its spirit as well.

Like Raphall, Einhorn was patriotic. He praised the United States, where Jews were allowed to live and worship in freedom. He said that every Jew "trembles for the preservation of the Union like a true son for the life of a dangerously sick mother." The difference between the two rabbis was that Einhorn was not willing to accept slavery in order to save the Union. Because of his views, his life was threatened and he was forced to leave Baltimore.

David Einhorn

*Maximilian
Michelbacher*

Bernhard Felsenthal was an abolitionist who had once refused a rabbinical post in Alabama because he felt he could not live in a slave state. He was deeply influenced by David Einhorn, and as a rabbi in Chicago he gave many anti-slavery sermons. Although he refused to condemn southern Jews who supported the Confederacy and slavery, he argued that "if anyone, it is the Jews above all others who should have the most burning and irreconcilable hatred" for slavery.

Bernhard Felsenthal

Maximilian Michelbacher, spiritual leader of Beth Ahabah Congregation in Richmond, Virginia, believed that slavery had been established and approved by God. In a wartime prayer for the preservation of the Confederacy, he spoke of "the man servants and maid servants Thou has given unto us, that we may rule over them. . . ."

Sabato Morais

Samuel M. Isaacs of New York was a rabbi and editor of *The Jewish Messenger*. He was also a strong supporter of the Union: "We are not citizens of the North or of the South, we are not republicans or democrats, but loyal citizens of that great republic, which has ever extended a welcome to the oppressed and has ever protected Israel."

Samuel M. Isaacs

Italian-born Sabato Morais was a rabbi in Philadelphia, known for his pro-Union sermons. He viewed the United States as a great experiment in democracy and was concerned that if it was destroyed over the issue of slavery, the future of democracy throughout the world would be in danger. Although he did not believe in slavery, Morais opposed both the abolitionists and the Southern defenders of slavery because he feared they would pull the Union apart. He argued that "We must have peace, but not at the cost of our national existence." Morais was a founder of the Jewish Theological Seminary.

Michael Heilprin was a Jewish scholar and editor of the *New American Cyclopaedia*. He was afraid that people would mistake Raphall's views for an official Jewish position on slavery, and would think that the "God of the Jews" was a "God of slavery." He attacked Raphall for taking the Bible literally, and reminded him of the many contradictions that later rabbis sought to interpret and explain.

Isaac Mayer Wise

Michael Heilprin

Rabbi Isaac Mayer Wise, editor of *The Israelite* in Cincinnati, was opposed to slavery, but was willing to accept it in order to save the Union. He called the abolitionists "fanatics," and was convinced that they were responsible for the outbreak of the Civil War.

James Koppel Gutheim was a rabbi in New Orleans. Although he was against slavery, he supported the Confederacy. When New Orleans was captured by Northern troops, he refused to take an oath of allegiance to the Union. He closed his synagogue for the rest of the war and he and many of his congregants left New Orleans. Gutheim was a member of the American Society for Promoting National Unity, the organization that sponsored Raphall's speech about slavery.

Isaac Leeser

James Koppel Gutheim

Prussian-born Isaac Leeser lived for a while in Richmond, Virginia. Those years may have made him more understanding of the southern point of view. Leeser became spiritual leader of Mikveh Israel in Philadelphia and was founder of the Jewish monthly magazine, *The Occident*. He was reluctant to discuss political questions and preferred to lead general prayers for peace and harmony. Leeser was sorry that Raphall had given a sermon about slavery, but admitted that he agreed with most of what Raphall had said.

CLOSE-UPS:
The Growth of Jewish Communities

MASSACHUSETTS

Moses Michael Hays lived in Massachusetts in the eighteenth century, but the generally unfriendly reception given Jews did not encourage many to settle there. There was no permanent Jewish community until Congregation Ohabei Shalom was established in Boston in 1842. The United Hebrew Benevolent Association was founded in 1864 and a Hebrew Ladies Sewing Society in 1878.

The Boston Jewish community grew with the mass migrations of the late nineteenth and early twentieth centuries. In 1875, there were only about three thousand Jews in the city; by 1939, there were one hundred sixty thousand.

In the second half of the nineteenth century, there were also Jewish communities in other Massachusetts cities, including Pittsfield, Worcester, Holyoke, and Springfield.

Boston's first synagogue, a wooden building on Warren Street, was erected in the 1850s.

TENNESSEE

The oldest Jewish communities in Tennessee are in Memphis and Nashville. A German-Jewish immigrant named David Hart was known to be living in Memphis in 1838. Ten years later, land was purchased for a cemetery. In 1850, a Hebrew Benevolent Society was formed and in 1854, B'nai Israel Congregation was chartered. Its first spiritual leader was Jacob Peres, who came to this country from Holland.

Congregation Khal Kodesh Mogen David was established in Nashville in 1853.

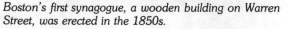

Jacob Joseph Peres and his wife, Eva Chuts Peres, arrived in Memphis in 1858. Peres served as spiritual leader, cantor, shoḥet, and head of the B'nai Israel religious school. He later became a lawyer, and in 1865 he was elected president of the Memphis School Board.

CALIFORNIA

Jews were among the forty-niners who came to San Francisco during the gold-rush years. They came both to look for gold and to sell supplies to prospectors. Among the most successful of the pioneer merchants was Levi Strauss, who became a millionaire selling popular work pants called "Levi's."

In 1849, there were enough Jews in the city to conduct two Yom Kippur services. Polish and English Jews met in a tent on Jackson Street. German Jews gathered on the second floor of a building on Montgomery Street. By 1851, the first group had founded Congregation Shearith Israel and the second, Congregation Emanu-El.

In 1854, about thirty Jews in Los Angeles formed the Hebrew Benevolent Society, a charitable organization. In 1866, the community hired Abraham Edelman as its *shoḥet* (ritual butcher), *mohel* (circumciser), and teacher. B'nai B'rith Congregation built the first synagogue in Los Angeles in 1873, on what is now South Broadway.

Right: An early advertisement for Levi's work pants. Below: The Pescadero and San Mateo Stage Company, owned by the firm of Levy Brothers, provided transportation over the California frontier.

MINNESOTA

In the 1850s, Jews were among the founders of Minnesota. John J. Noah was the secretary of the state's constitutional convention. Most of the early Jewish settlers in St. Paul were of German origin and were merchants or fur traders. Community life was already well-organized by 1856, when two small congregations merged to become Mount Zion Hebrew Congregation.

A typical early settler in St. Paul was Julius Austrian, who arrived in the winter of 1851, his dogsled filled with merchandise to sell. He and his wife Hannah settled permanently in the city in the late 1860s. Hannah Austrian founded the first Jewish women's group in St. Paul, the Mount Zion Hebrew Ladies Benevolent Society.

In Minneapolis, Congregation Shaarai Tov, later called Temple Israel, was established in 1878.

In the 1850s, Joseph Ullmann of St. Paul traded in liquor, cigars, and fur. His wife, Amelia, wrote in her memoirs that Minnesota's winters were so harsh she had to wrap herself in buffalo hides to keep warm.

Otto Mears (center) came to Colorado from Lithuania. He was known as the "Pathfinder of San Juan" because of the roads and railroads he built through the San Juan Mountains in the southwestern part of Colorado. In 1868, Mears negotiated a treaty with Chief Ouray (right) of the Colorado Utes.

COLORADO

The Jewish community in Denver was founded by pioneers who came to Colorado to participate in the 1859 gold rush. There were Jews in almost every mining camp, and by 1866, there were more than a hundred Jews in Denver alone. Notable Colorado Jews include Simon Guggenheim, who was a U.S. senator from 1907 to 1913, and Frances Wisebart Jacobs, "the Queen of Charities," who helped found the Charity Organization Society in Denver in 1887.

ARIZONA

Many Jews came to Arizona after the discovery of gold in 1862. As in California, most of the Jewish pioneers opened stores in the mining camps. There were also Jews who ran mining operations, such as Leopold Ephraim of Nogales and Henry Lesinsky, owner of the Longfellow Mine in the San Francisco Mountains.

The first organized Jewish community life in the state was at Tombstone, where Yom Kippur services were held in 1881. Tombstone was also the home of one of the most notorious Jewish women in the American West, Josephine Sarah Marcus, who lived with Sheriff Wyatt Earp for more than fifty years.

Among prominent Arizona Jews were Nathan Benjamin Appel, a delegate to the First Arizona Territorial Legislature in 1863; Herman Bendell, who came to Phoenix in 1871 as commissioner of Indian affairs; and Michael and Joseph Goldwasser, who changed their name to Goldwater and opened the first of what became a chain of stores across the state.

"Big Mike" Goldwater, grandfather of Arizona senator and 1964 presidential candidate, Barry Goldwater.

Life on the southwestern frontier was not without its dangers. This sketch shows the body of a Phoenix butcher, Marcus Goldbaum, who was murdered by Apache Indians while prospecting in the Whetstone Mountains in 1886.

FLORIDA

Moses Elias Levy, a Moroccan Jew, came to Florida in 1821, the year the Spaniards gave it to the United States. He developed plantations in northern Florida, but was never successful in attracting settlers to the area. Levy County in Florida was named after him. Colonel Abraham C. Myers of South Carolina served in the Florida Indian Wars of 1836–38 and 1841–42. Fort Myers was named after him.

Jacksonville was the site of the first organized Jewish community in Florida. There were Jews in the city as early as the 1850s and Congregation Ahavath Chesed was established in 1867.

Samuel Singer and Isidor Cohen, who came to Miami at the end of the nineteenth century, were among its first Jewish settlers. By 1930, the Jewish population of the city had reached three thousand five hundred. Hordes of tourists began to descend upon Florida each winter, and the number of residents grew dramatically. By the 1980s, there were hundreds of thousands of Jews living in Florida, among them many retirees from the North.

Isidor Cohen, Miami pioneer.

Duval Street in Key West, Florida, in the early 1900s. Louis Wolfson, whose store is shown on the left, was a city commissioner.

IV · YEARS OF MASS MIGRATION

לֶךְ־לְךָ מֵאַרְצְךָ וּמִמּוֹלַדְתְּךָ וּמִבֵּית אָבִיךָ
אֶל־הָאָרֶץ אֲשֶׁר אַרְאֶךָּ.

"Go forth from your native land and from your kindred and from your father's house
to the land that I will show you."
Genesis 12:1

In 1880, there were about two hundred eighty thousand Jews in the United States. Some could trace their ancestry to the Sephardim who came here in the seventeenth and eighteenth centuries. The majority were from families

Above: A shipload of immigrants coming to America in the early 1900s.

that came to America in the first half of the nineteenth century, from the lands of central Europe.

Between 1880 and 1925, more than two million Jews emigrated to America. These newcomers were very different from the established community of assimilated American Jews. They brought with them the languages, culture, and religious practices of the Eastern European lands from which most of them came.

It takes courage to migrate from one nation to another. When the Lord told Abraham to go from Ḥaran to the promised land of Canaan, Abraham had to leave behind his country, his relatives, and his father's house. In the same way, the Jews who came to live in America left behind their loved ones and the lands of their birth. They set out on long and difficult journeys. They crossed borders illegally. Some of them never again saw their friends and families.

Why did these millions of Jewish immigrants risk everything to come to America? What kind of life did they make for themselves here? How did their coming change the face of Jewish life in the United States?

Jewish passengers being registered by officials of the Hamburg-American shipping line (1909). Many immigrants left Europe through the German port of Hamburg.

CHAPTER ONE
WHY THEY CAME TO AMERICA

Several million Jews journeyed to America during the age of mass migration. They came here to escape from the horrors of anti-Semitism, to avoid unfair military draft laws, and to find a better life than was possible for them and their families in the old country.

Escape from Anti-Semitism

In 1881, the Russian czar, Alexander II, was assassinated. The government attempted to protect itself from the possibility of revolution by blaming the Jews for the nation's problems. Rumors were spread that the Jews were responsible for the czar's death and

there were numerous anti-Jewish riots, called pogroms. Jews were attacked, raped, and murdered, and their property was looted and burned. Government officials, including the police, rarely did anything to stop the pogroms or to protect the Jews. In some communities, Jewish self-defense groups were formed, but these usually were poorly armed and ineffective.

These terrorist attacks of the 1880s were accompanied by discriminatory laws designed to force the Jews to convert, emigrate, or starve. Among these were laws restricting the areas in which Jews could live, preventing them from attending universities, and forbidding them to work on Sundays or Christian holidays.

Jewish victims of a Russian pogrom.

Waves of Pogroms

A second series of pogroms occurred between the years 1903 and 1907. Among the worst of these was the Kishinev pogrom, which took place on April 6–7, 1903. Over five thousand Russian soldiers were stationed in the city, but they did nothing to protect the helpless Jewish population. Forty-nine Jews were killed and more than five hundred were injured. Thirteen hundred Jewish homes and businesses were destroyed and two thousand Jews were left homeless.

In October 1905, there were pogroms in more than six hundred fifty Russian cities and towns. Within a few days, more than eight hundred Jews were killed. In Odessa alone, there were over three hundred dead and thousands injured.

Between 1917 and 1921, the years of the Russian Revolution, the pogroms were even more violent. It is estimated that over sixty thousand Jews were killed and three times as many wounded.

It is no wonder that over two million Jews left Russia. The largest number of them came to America.

The bodies of Jews murdered during the Kishinev pogrom.

A Jewish woman views the wreckage of the Kishinev pogrom.

A group of fusgeyers *stop to rest during their long protest-walk across Europe.*

Anti-Semitism in Rumania

The situation of the Jews in Rumania was also very difficult. Towards the end of the nineteenth century, their citizenship was taken away; they were expelled from certain parts of the country; they were forbidden to be lawyers or teachers; they could not trade in salt, tobacco, or alcohol; and they were not allowed to attend public schools. Between 1881 and 1914, over seventy-five thousand Rumanian Jews came to the United States, representing almost 30 percent of the Jewish population of Rumania. Among them were the *fusgeyers* (walkers), who left Rumania on foot and

marched across Europe to call attention to the anti-Semitism in their country. These spirited young people sang songs, conducted rallies, and published newspapers as they walked to Hamburg, Germany. From there, they took ships to Great Britain, the United States, and Canada.

Ḥotin, a small town that was sometimes part of Rumania, sometimes part of Russia. This street scene is typical of the towns in which many eastern-European Jews lived.

Military Service

Many young men came to America to avoid military service in their native lands. This was not because they were afraid to serve, but because being in the military meant having to eat *traif* (non-kosher) food and violating the Sabbath.

There was also discrimination against Jews in the military. In some countries, Jewish soldiers could not be promoted. In Russia, the situation was even worse. Jewish boys as young as eight years old were forced into the czar's army for twenty-five years of service. Some were tortured until they agreed to convert to Christianity. While Jewish civilians were being deprived of their rights, their sons were being kidnapped by the military and torn from their Jewish heritage. Could they be blamed for not wanting to sacrifice their lives to defend a country that treated them so cruelly?

The Jews of the Turkish empire also had to deal with forced military service. To avoid the draft, young Jewish men left Turkey and Syria (which was then part of the empire) and came to America.

Jewish soldiers in the Polish army.

Yahrzeit at the Front, a lithograph made during the Franco-Prussian War by the German-Jewish artist Mortiz Oppenheim, shows Jews as soldiers in a European army.

Economic Conditions

The period of the mass migrations was an era of depressions, wars, and revolutions that ruined the economy of Europe. The Jews were affected more than other peoples. Many of the Jews of Eastern Europe lived in unbelievable poverty. In small villages and towns, some of them lived in one-room hovels with dirt floors. Their suffering was increased by anti-semitic laws that restricted the ways they could make a living.

The economy in eastern Mediterranean countries was also disrupted by wars and revolutions. In Syria, the Jews were affected by the opening of the Suez Canal in 1869. The canal diverted much of the trade that used to go through the Syrian city of Aleppo. As Aleppo declined, its Jewish bankers and merchants lost their livelihoods.

A Russian-Jewish woman, her children, and their simple home in an impoverished area of eastern Europe.

Small-town life in eastern Europe.

Immigrants getting their first view of the Statue of Liberty.

"Di Goldeneh Medina"

America was said to be *di goldeneh medina*, the golden land. It was supposed to be the place where you could get anything you wanted or needed. One immigrant who sent a ticket to his brother in Europe said, "I brought my brother Jake up to America." His use of the word "up" is a direct translation of the Hebrew word *aliyah*, meaning emigration to the promised land. In Hebrew, one "goes up" to the land of Israel. For the immigrants, America had become the new promised land, where they hoped to find a better life for themselves and for their children.

The world they left behind (clockwise from top left): Jewish musicians; a couple from Turkey; a Zionist youth group in Poland; an old man from a small town in Poland; Jews from Rhodes.

Top left: Children in a Jewish school. Top right: Jewish revolutionaries in Russia. Center: Market day in a small town in Eastern Europe. Bottom: Jewish socialists mourn victims killed during a political demonstration.

CLOSE-UPS: *The Decision to Come*

Celia Weiss Schwartz

A WOMAN ALONE IN MISKOLC, HUNGARY

Celia Weiss Schwartz was living in Hungary with her two young children after her husband, Farkas, had died. Her stepdaughter, Rebish, had gone to America several years before. "Come to us," Rebish wrote. "We will help you."

Celia was a woman alone. Could she travel across Europe by herself with two small children? Would they be safe on the boat to America, with no man to protect them?

But she was a penniless widow and knew her children would not have much of a future if they stayed in Hungary. So, in 1891, Celia gathered her courage, traveled to Hamburg, Germany, boarded the S.S. Dania, and took her children to America.

Celia's children, Jennie and Adolf.

A *FUSGEYER* FROM VASLUI, RUMANIA

In 1900, Leon Finkelstein left Rumania with the *fusgeyers* who marched through Europe to protest the treatment of Jews in their native land.

The Finkelstein family had personal experience with the government's anti-semitism. Leon's father Koppel was involved in a lawsuit with a non-Jew over ownership of the family's orchard. The judge purposely set the trial for *Shabbat*, knowing that as an observant Jew, Koppel would be unable to come to court. Because of his failure to appear, the family lost its orchard.

Leon went to the synagogue to say goodbye to his grandfather Yossel Leibovici, but the old man would not allow him to interrupt the service. After prayers were over, Yossel got on a horse and rode out of town after his grandson, to bless him and kiss him goodbye.

Leon walked across Europe, ending up in England. He took a boat to North America and settled in Canada. In 1922, his son Samuel went to the United States, seeking greater economic opportunity. Soon after, Leon the *fusgeyer* joined his son and settled in this country.

Leon Finkelstein

A MOTHER LEAVES HER CHILDREN TO SEARCH FOR HER HUSBAND

Isidore Goldberger came to America in 1898 from Hungary. He left behind his pregnant wife Celia and their three children. After several years, he stopped writing to his family. In 1905, Celia heard that Isidore was working in a hat factory in Orange, New Jersey, and that he was seeing another woman. Determined to

Jacob Waxman

Bella Waxman

Celia Goldberger and her children, soon after they were reunited in America.

save her marriage, she left her youngest children with relatives in Hungary, and came to America with her fifteen-year-old son Harry to look for her husband.

Celia went to every hat factory in Orange until she found Isidore. Reunited, the two of them opened a restaurant. Isidore died in 1909. Celia and Harry continued to run the restaurant. By 1912, they had saved enough money to bring the rest of the family to America.

The younger children did not know their father, who had left Hungary when they were still babies. They resented their mother because they felt that she had abandoned them. The only person they trusted was their brother Harry. When they came to America, he met them at the boat. Harry helped them to adjust to life in America and supported them while they went to school.

ESCAPING THE RUSSIAN POGROMS

Jacob Waxman was a cabinet-maker and a free-thinker. He did not believe in religion and did not consider himself an orthodox Jew. But in a small town like Kalarash, he had to go to synagogue and observe Jewish customs or people would talk.

In 1905, Jacob decided to go to America to escape small-town life. His wife, Bella, wanted to stay in Kalarash with their children, Isidore and Ḥaika. Their marriage had been arranged by their families, and they agreed to a friendly divorce. Eventually, Bella remarried.

Later that year, there was a bloody pogrom in Kalarash. Fifty-four Jews were murdered and countless others were beaten, robbed, and raped. Hundreds of homes were destroyed by fire. Bella and her children escaped by running to the station where, luckily, a train was waiting. They lay on the floor of the train as it left Kalarash and the pogrom.

In 1906, Isidore was old enough to be drafted into the army. Bella suggested that he cut off his trigger finger to avoid the draft. Instead, he persuaded her to allow him to go to his father in America.

"Today is quiet, tomorrow a pogrom," Jacob wrote, pleading with Bella to allow their daughter, Ḥaika, to leave Russia. Bella finally agreed, and in 1907 her second husband took Ḥaika to America. Bella stayed behind, continuing to run her inn. When she was sure her husband could make a living in America, she sold the inn and joined him.

Isidore and Ḥaika in a photograph sent to Jacob in America, to show him they had survived the Kalarash pogrom.

Jacob and Esther Angel with their children.

A CITY IN FLAMES

After they were expelled from Spain in 1492, members of the Angel family came to Salonika, in Greece. In 1553, an estimated twenty thousand Jews lived in the city. Most of them, like the Angels, spoke Judeo-Spanish (Ladino) at home, using French or Spanish to conduct their business.

In 1916, Jacob and Esther Angel were afraid that their son Salamon would be drafted into the Greek army, so they sent him to America with his aunt and uncle. Salamon traveled at the height of World War I. His ship had to dodge German submarines as it crossed the Atlantic.

Salonika was destroyed by fire in 1917. Over fifty thousand of the city's eighty thousand Jews lost their homes. The Angels went to Alexandria, Egypt, where they lived for a few years before coming to America. Their married daughter, Sol, remained in Salonika and died in 1924. Her husband and two children were killed in the Holocaust.

AVOIDING THE CZAR'S ARMY

Shimon and Feiga Waltman Goodman lived in a village near Novoselitsa in Russia. Five of their seven children were boys and Feiga was afraid that they would be kidnapped and forced into the czar's army. In 1914, when their oldest son Yonkel was sixteen, Feiga and Shimon decided to send him to his uncle in America.

The Russian government did not want to lose potential soldiers like Yonkel, so it refused to grant him a passport or exit permit. Yonkel tried to sneak across the border. He was discovered by border guards who shot at him as he ran from Russia to Rumania. But he

made it, and Yonkel finally entered the United States with false papers that declared him a citizen of Rumania.

World War I and the Russian Revolution prevented the family from joining Yonkel in America. In 1918, Novoselitsa became part of Rumania. Shimon got a Rumanian passport and came to America. By 1920, he and Yonkel had earned enough money to bring over Feiga and the children. Within a year, Feiga was dead. Bella, ten years old, now had to take care of her five brothers and her baby sister.

Shimon and Feiga Goodman with six of their children and a cousin (rear).

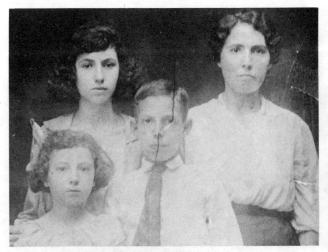

Esther Levy with three of her children.

Hersh Eliah Wiesenthal with his daughter Ḥana, her husband Yitzḥak Herzog, and their children.

NO WAY TO EARN A LIVING

Yoshua and Esther Levy were members of the Sephardic community in Istanbul. Their ancestors had arrived in Turkey soon after the expulsion from Spain and the family honored its heritage by continuing to speak Judeo-Spanish (Ladino).

The Levys were a religious family. Yoshua's father had gone to Palestine because he wanted to die "in his own land." Esther read Hebrew and Yoshua was educated in Jewish law. This did not help him make a living in Istanbul, so in 1910 he went to Cuba, leaving his family behind. He served as ḥazan in a Cuban synagogue and supported himself by selling cloth.

In 1916, Esther was lonely and sold their house in Istanbul to raise money for tickets. She took her children to join Yoshua in Cuba. She did not like life on the island. In the years that followed, she and the children commuted between New York and Cuba while Yoshua remained in Cuba. In 1921, the family settled permanently in New York.

"AMERICA IS A *TRAIF* COUNTRY"

Shmuel and Yankel Wiesenthal had gone to America. They wanted the rest of their family to join them. But Hersh Eliah and Ethel Wiesenthal, their parents, were not sure. Life in Skala, in the Austro-Hungarian Empire, was not easy. The family was poor and Hersh Eliah had lost his job.

The deciding factor was the family's commitment to traditional Judaism. Hersh Eliah spent every day at the Chortkover synagogue in Skala, praying and studying Torah. Ethel was a *zogerkeh*, a woman who knew Hebrew and who led the other women in prayers at shul. She was so religious that she did not want to go to America because the boat trip took twelve days and she refused to travel on Shabbat.

Their other children, Hana and Feivish, also chose to stay in Europe. "America is a *traif* [non-kosher]

country," they said. They thought it would be impossible to lead a traditional Jewish life there.

Hersh Eliah's brother Zeḥariah had gone to New York in 1904, but he never intended to stay. He wanted to earn enough money to live well in Skala and he returned there in 1907.

Ethel died in 1915, Hersh Eliah in 1933. Every other member of the family who remained in Europe perished in the Holocaust.

Zeḥariah Wiesenthal in New York, 1905.

Feivish Wiesenthal with his children, Alter and Ethel.

Avraham, Malka, Leah, and Mechal Grinovezer.

Gedaliah Khenvin

NO TICKETS TO AMERICA

Mechal Grinovezer was a rabbi who did not like to earn money in the service of God. To support his family he worked as a sugar broker. It was difficult for him to make a living in Ḥotin, Rumania, so in the early 1920s, the family decided to go to America. Malka wrote to an uncle in New York, asking that he sponsor her family. She hoped that he would send her money for tickets and help Mechal get a job in America.

Malka's uncle was a practical man. He told her that there were more than enough rabbis in America. He did not see how Mechal would be able to support his family in America any better than in Ḥotin. At least in Rumania, Mechal knew the language. Malka's uncle urged her not to come to America.

Malka's daughter Leah wrote to her cousin Shraga Gottesfeld in Palestine and asked him to help her make *aliyah* (emigrate) to the Holy Land. Shraga paid for her ticket and Leah traveled alone to Palestine.

Malka, Mechal, and their son Avraham were killed by the Nazis. Leah, her three children and her grandchildren live in Ḥaifa, Israel.

Leah Grinovezer Golan, her children and several grandchildren in Haifa, in 1980.

WAR AND REVOLUTION SEPARATE A FAMILY

In May 1914, Max Khenvin left Russia with his two oldest daughters. He hoped they would earn enough money to send for his wife Leah and their four younger children by August. His plans were thwarted by the outbreak of World War I that summer. Max sent money to support his family, but because of the war, he was unable to bring them to America.

In 1917, the Russian Revolution brought to the Ukraine a series of the worst pogroms in Russian history. The Khenvins hid in the field while *pogromchiks* destroyed their home. For the next three years, Leah and her children wandered on foot, hiding in barns and sleeping in fields as each town to which they walked was attacked by *pogromchiks*. Because Max had no idea where they were, they had no money. Most of their meals consisted of bread and tea. Skinny and sick, they finally made their way to Leah's aunt in Kremenchug, in the Ukraine. From there, they were able to contact Max in America.

Leah's fourteen-year-old son, Gedaliah, joined the city's Jewish self-defense organization. The group had no money. Its members wore fake guns and home-made uniforms. They thought they might be able to protect the city's Jews by scaring the *pogromchiks*.

In 1921, Max became an American citizen. Leah and the children in Russia were included in his naturalization papers. It took two more years for the visas and passage money to arrive in Russia. When Leah and the children came to New York, they were in such bad health that they would not have been admitted to this country if they had not already been American citizens.

FROM OUR JEWISH HERITAGE:
The Jewish Family

The decision to come to America often meant the break-up of Jewish families. Sons and daughters never saw their parents again. Perhaps this process of separation was partly responsible for the weakening of traditional Judaism among many immigrants to America. What does our Jewish heritage teach us about the role of the Jewish family?

In biblical times, family ties were extremely important. This drawing shows the reunion of brothers Jacob and Esau and their families. (Genesis 33:4)

The Family of Israel

The importance of the family to Jewish life is apparent from the ancient beginnings of Jewish history. Most of the book of Genesis is the story of the first family of Israel: of our fathers Abraham, Isaac, and Jacob, and our mothers, Sarah, Rebecca, Leah, and Rachel. It tells of the sons of Jacob and of their life-style of large, extended families living together.

Throughout the Bible, people are identified by their parents and often by their tribes as well. Numerous sections of the Bible are family records: a series of marriage, birth, and death announcements that would fascinate a genealogist. Indeed, as the Bible notes, ". . . all Israel was registered by genealogies." (I Chronicles 9:1)

The reason for this emphasis on family is that God's covenant was with Abraham and his seed, or children. (Genesis 17:7-8) It was to Abraham's descendants that the land was promised, to them that the commandments were given. We are told to honor our fathers and mothers (Exodus 20:12) because it is through them that we inherit the legacy of Israel and by them that we are taught about our heritage. (Proverbs 1:8)

Marriage: "When I found him whom my soul loves . . . . I held him and would not let him go" (Song of Songs 3:4)

The Jewish Family at Home

When a Jewish couple marries, they stand under a *ḥupah* (marriage canopy). This symbolizes the home that they will make together, in which will take place many of the most important rituals of Jewish observance.

Each meal eaten in a Jewish home is an event rich with Jewish tradition. The kinds of food that may be eaten and the manner of their preparations are outlined in the laws of *kashrut*. The prayers before and after the meal thank God for providing the food. On the Sabbath and holidays, *kiddush*, the prayer recited over a cup of wine, marks the special holiness of the meal. On Pesaḥ, the *seder* takes place at the dinner table. During Sukkot, the meals are eaten in a booth, in remembrance of the temporary homes in which the Hebrews lived while wandering in Sinai.

In the traditional Jewish home, candles are lit on Shabbat and holidays. In celebration of Ḥanukah, a *ḥanukiah* (Ḥanukah lamp) shines in the window. The words of God are in the *mezuzah* on the doorpost (Deuteronomy 11:20) and the parents follow the commandment to "teach them to your children." (Deuteronomy 11:19)

The Jewish home is the center of Jewish life. It is through strong family ties and a commitment to tradition in the home that Jewish heritage is preserved.

Kiddush: "Blessed are you, O Lord our God, king of the universe, who created the fruit of the vine."

Shabbat: "Remember the sabbath day, to keep it holy." (Exodus 20:8)

Circumcision: "So shall my covenant be in your flesh an everlasting covenant." (Genesis 17:13)

Education: "Train a child in the way he should go and even when he is old, he will not depart from it." (Proverbs 22:6)

Bar and Bat Mitzvah: "Whoever teaches his child teaches not only his child but also his child's child, and so on to the end of generations." (Talmud)

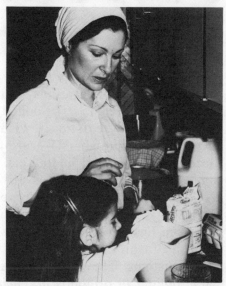

Kashrut: "And thou shalt eat and be satisfied, and bless the Lord thy God." (Deuteronomy 8:10)

Generations Together: "One who learns from the aged, to what is he like? To one that eats ripe grapes and drinks old wine." (Talmud)

CHAPTER TWO
THEIR RECEPTION IN AMERICA

Liberty Beckons

On the base of the Statue of Liberty is a poem by Emma Lazarus, a Sephardic Jew whose ancestors had lived in America since the eighteenth century. Although Emma Lazarus worked among the immigrants and was personally sympathetic to their plight, her words unintentionally reveal the true feelings of the existing Jewish-American community to the newest Jewish immigrants. In her poem, Lazarus referred to the immigrants as "tired . . . poor . . . huddled masses" and, in a final telling phrase, described them as "wretched refuse." It was a nice way of describing the newcomers as people that nobody wanted.

Immigrants gazing at the Statue of Liberty.

Emma Lazarus. The final paragraph of her poem, "The New Colossus," reads as follows: "Give me your tired, your poor/Your huddled masses yearning to breathe free/The wretched refuse of your teeming shore./Send these, the homeless, tempest-tost to me./I lift my lamp beside the golden door."

A Clash of Cultures

During the mass migrations, hundreds of thousands of foreign Jews flooded the ports of America. The existing Jewish community, called "uptowners," were largely of German background, middle class and assimilated. Most were conservative in politics and Reform in religious practice. The immigrants, or "downtowners," were usually from Eastern Europe. They were poor, with old-fashioned clothes and old-fashioned customs. They were sometimes radical in politics or orthodox in religion. Apart from their shared ancient heritage, the German Jews had little in common with these mostly Russian newcomers.

By the turn of the century, Jews whose families had arrived during or before the 1840s spoke English, were assimilated, and looked like other Americans. Their immigrant counterparts usually spoke Yiddish and wore old-fashioned clothing.

Many native-born American women such as these thought they had little in common with the newcomers. Some immigrant women could not read or write, even in their native language. They might spend long hours at work for low pay, while their uptown counterparts were at school or doing charity work.

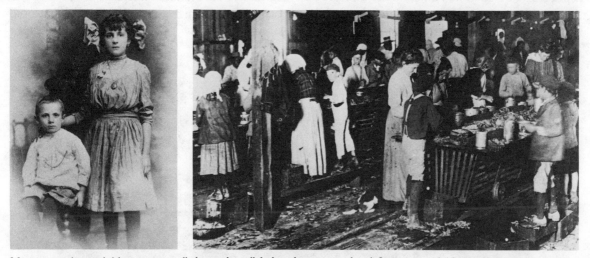

Most native-born children were well-dressed, well-fed and went to school. Immigrant children often were often hungry, and badly-clothed. Some had to work to help support their families.

Their Reception in America 115

While not all Jews already in America were rich, most were fairly comfortable. Often they had their own businesses, such as this retail store in Richmond, Virginia. In contrast, newcomers usually worked as peddlers or in factories.

The uptown Jews realized that the huge numbers of the immigrants would ultimately turn the German-Jewish majority into a minority, and that they would lose control of Jewish community life. They were also afraid that these visible, vocal, and obviously foreign Jews would cause other Americans to become anti-Semitic. In addition, the Germans knew that the poverty of these Russian Jews would place a great strain on Jewish-American charitable organizations. An example of this view was the report of one Jewish charity that described the immigrants as "a curse" to the established American Jewish community.

The Uptowners Take Charge

In spite of their misgivings, American Jews did take care of their own. They set up organizations to meet the immigrants when they landed and help them through immigration formalities. They established settlement houses and schools in which immigrants were taught English and rules of citizenship, and were given job training. They provided financial assistance and gave medical care to those in need.

The German Jews had little understanding of the foreigners' heritage and were eager to Americanize them. At the Educational Alliance, a New York center for immigrant

For newcomers who spoke no English, immigration formalities could be quite frightening.

Young immigrant girls learning to sew at the Jewish Manual Training School in Chicago, 1892.

education, the uptown sponsers conducted classes only in English. They considered Yiddish an inferior form of German.

The proud newcomers regarded the Germans as snobbish and unsympathetic. They began to set up their own self-help organizations. As one immigrant put it, he and other Russian Jews preferred to help themselves rather than be "insulted by our proud [German] brethren to whom a Russian Jew is a *schnorrer* [beggar], a tramp, a good-for-nothing." These self-help societies were a continuation of the old Jewish traditions of mutual responsibility and *tzedakah* (charity).

Proud graduates of a citizenship course display the American flag.

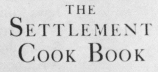

THE
SETTLEMENT
COOK BOOK

Compiled by
MRS. SIMON KANDER

Tested Recipes from
The Settlement Cooking Classes
The Milwaukee Public School Kitchens
The School of Trades for Girls
and Experienced Housewives

♡

Twenty-third Edition
Enlarged and Revised

The Settlement Cook Book Co.
MILWAUKEE, WIS.

The Settlement Cookbook, *compiled by Lizzie Kander for the Abraham Lincoln Settlement House of Milwaukee, contained recipes tested in the cooking classes for immigrants.*

Shearith Israel, the Spanish-Portuguese synagogue in New York, completed its new building on Central Park West and West 70th Street in 1897.

The Sephardic Experience

Although the vast majority of the newcomers were from Central and Eastern Europe, there were also between thirty thousand and fifty thousand Sephardic immigrants. These people were descended from Jews who, after being expelled from Spain and Portugal at the end of the fifteenth century, went to countries in the eastern Mediterranean, such as Turkey, Greece, and Syria.

Within the Sephardic community, there were similar misunderstandings between immigrants and native American Jews. The members of Shearith Israel, the Spanish-Portuguese Synagogue in New York, were fully assimilated Americans. Some of them were descended from people who came to this country in the 1600s. They were bewildered by the energetic new arrivals, who spoke a medieval form of Spanish known as Judeo-Spanish or Ladino.

The new Sephardim had a hard time adjusting to life in America. Because they did not know Yiddish, they did not fit in well with the Ashkenazic immigrants and could not easily get work in the Jewish-owned shops. The established Sephardim tried to help. They opened a synagogue and settlement house on the Lower East Side, where they taught English and job skills to the newcomers.

Like the Ashkenazim, the Sephardim eventually formed their own self-help societies. Immigrants from Salonika founded *Etz Ha-ḥayim* (Tree of Life), and *Rodefei Tsedek* (Seekers of Justice) was founded by Jews from Turkey and Syria.

Ashkenazic organizations also helped the Sephardim. In 1911, the Hebrew Immigrant Aid Society (HIAS) opened its "Oriental Bureau," headed by Moise Gadol, a Bulgarian Sephardic Jew who spoke Ladino. The Bureau was closed in 1915 because of lack of funds. HIAS continued to try to assist the Sephardim, but its efforts were limited by its staff's lack of knowledge of Sephardic culture and language.

Moise Salomon Gadol, head of the Oriental Bureau of HIAS, later became editor of the Judeo-Spanish newspaper, La America.

From the Eastern Seaports

Most of the immigrants stayed in the eastern cities where they had landed, with the largest number concentrated in New York's Lower East Side. In an attempt to relieve the crowded conditions of the cities' ghettos, German Jews founded the Industrial Removal Office in 1901. Its aim was to move immigrants to other American communities, mostly in the midwest. Over the next ten years, the IRO distributed more than sixty thousand immigrants throughout America. The IRO sent agents to these communities to find jobs and sponsors for the newcomers, and to organize local committees to help them to adjust.

A second method of dispersing the immigrants was the Galveston Plan. Rather than landing at eastern seaports, some immigrants were taken directly from Europe to Galveston, Texas. From there, they were sent to towns in the interior of the country. Between 1907 and 1912, about five thousand people were brought to America on the Galveston Plan.

Some immigrants found it hard to practice traditional Judaism outside the cities where there was no kosher meat or Hebrew schools. Others were dismayed by the limited educational and cultural life. Still others were lonely for the sounds of Yiddish and the company of fellow Jews. Many of the immigrants who were sent or went voluntarily to small-town America, later moved to the cities.

Jews who lived in small towns across northern Michigan hungered for each other's company and often got together in gatherings such as this 1908 reunion.

Agricultural Colonies

Another scheme to relieve the congestion of the cities was to turn the Eastern European Jew into a farmer. This plan was well received by some of the immigrants, particularly the members of the *Am Olam* (Eternal People) movement. They believed that the salvation of the Jewish people lay in a return to their agricultural roots. As one of the farmers put it, Jews should "become tillers of the soil and thus shake off the accusation that we are mere petty mercenaries, living upon the toil of others."

The Jewish agricultural colony at Cotopaxi, Colorado in the 1880s. One of the settlers described the area as "the poorest place in the world for farming—poor land, lots of rocks, and no water"

The members of *Am Olam* set up farming colonies at Sicily Island, Louisiana; New Odessa, Oregon; and Crémieux, South Dakota. With the help of such charitable organizations as the Baron de Hirsch Fund and the European-based Alliance Israélite Universelle, Jewish agricultural communities were also established in New Jersey, Colorado, Kansas, and North Dakota. Almost all the colonies failed, usually for a combination of reasons: Many of the immigrants had no training as farmers, and they often settled on land that was difficult to farm or located far from cities where they could sell their produce.

The most successful farming settlements were in southern New Jersey. These colonies did well primarily because they were near the Philadelphia and New York markets. They also had established an agricultural school to train the immigrants, and had set up other industries, such as the clothing and cigar factories at the Alliance colony, to supplement the farmers' income during hard times.

The Baron de Hirsch Agricultural School in Woodbine, New Jersey trained Jewish immigrants to be farmers. Left: Students work in the school's laboratory (1907).

Jewish women working at the canning factory in Norma, New Jersey, part of the Alliance colony (1907).

CLOSE-UPS:
Community Organizers and Organizations

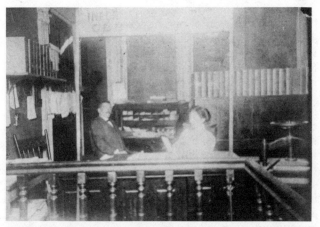

The HIAS bureau on Ellis Island.

HIAS, THE IMMIGRANTS' WELCOMING COMMITTEE

The Hebrew Immigrant Aid Society (HIAS) was formed in 1909 by the merger of several organizations whose purpose was to help newcomers to America. HIAS had Yiddish-speaking agents at Ellis Island and other American ports to guide arriving passengers through medical tests and other immigration formalities.

HIAS representatives defended those threatened with deportation, investigated complaints about conditions on the ships, provided food, housing and job counseling, and conducted classes in citizenship. They also paid transportation costs for immigrants destined for American communities outside of the port cities and reunited newcomers with their families in this country.

During its first ten years, HIAS helped over half a million Jewish immigrants. It has continued its work, lending assistance to new arrivals from the Soviet Union, Rumania, Iran, and South Vietnam.

A seder held by HIAS for immigrants on Ellis Island (1913).

THE BARON DE HIRSCH FUND

Baron Maurice de Hirsch of Germany believed that the future of the masses of poor Jews in Europe and the Middle East lay in education and a return to the land. He once wrote that "the Jews have not lost the agricultural qualities their forefathers possessed," and that he would "try to make for them a new home in different lands . . . as free farmers on their own soil."

The $2.5 million Baron de Hirsch Fund was founded in New York in 1891. The fund was intended to help immigrants get to America and to assist them in settling here. Together with de Hirsch's Jewish Colonization Association, the Fund established experimental agricultural colonies across the United States, founded schools, including an agricultural school in Woodbine, New Jersey, and sponsored Jewish immigrants who were willing to become American farmers. The Fund also opened the Hebrew Technical Institute on the Lower East Side, a night school that taught boys such crafts as cabinetmaking and tinsmithing.

The sign-painting department of a Baron de Hirsch Fund trade school.

A CHARITABLE GERMAN MILLIONAIRE

Jacob Henry Schiff, a millionaire banker and philanthropist, was a leader of the uptown Jews who was also respected by the immigrants. A member of Temple Emanuel, Schiff had received a traditional religious education in his native Germany. Although he felt sympathy to the needs of the downtown Jews, he also wanted to Americanize them.

Schiff raised funds for the Jewish Theological Seminary, the rabbinical school of the Conservative

Jacob Schiff and his wife, Theresa.

JUDAH MAGNES AND THE KEHILLAH

Although Judah Leib Magnes was born in San Francisco, he had traveled in Europe and was respectful of the European Jewish way of life. He felt that the immigrants should become loyal to America, but that they should also keep their own language, culture, history, and traditions.

Magnes endeared himself to the immigrants when he led a demonstration of one hundred fifty thousand Jews protesting the 1905 pogroms and raised money for Russian-Jewish self-defense groups. He was a founder and the first president of the New York Kehillah. The Kehillah, established in 1908, was an umbrella organization of Jewish societies and institutions. It was an attempt to unify the Jewish community. It fought crime on the Lower East Side, published textbooks, and was active in labor arbitration. It provided a link between uptown and downtown Jews.

A committed Zionist, Magnes emigrated to Palestine in 1922 and was a founder of Hebrew University in Jerusalem. Without his leadership, the Kehillah experiment eventually failed.

movement. He regarded this movement as a more American form of Judaism than that of the orthodox immigrants, and hoped that many of them would join it. He also supported the Educational Alliance, the Hebrew Technical School, and the Galveston Plan, all of which he felt would help move the immigrants into mainstream America.

Schiff's devotion to the Jewish people also influenced his business decisions. Horrified by the Russian government's anti-Semitism, he helped sponsor a $200 million bond issue to aid the Japanese during the Russo-Japanese War. He tried to block attempts by the Russian government to get loans from the world financial community. He also gave money to Russian-Jewish self-defense groups and organized the Russian Refugee Relief and Colonization Fund.

Judah Leib Magnes

When Schiff learned that the immigrant sculptor, Jules Leon Butensky, had been evicted from his Lower East Side tenement, he commissioned him to do this statue, Universal Peace. *The statue illustrates the words of the prophet Isaiah, "and they shall beat their swords into plowshares." (Isaiah 2:4)*

THE NATIONAL COUNCIL OF JEWISH WOMEN

Founded in Chicago in 1893 by Hannah G. Solomon, the National Council of Jewish Women was made up mostly of women of German-Jewish backgrounds who were pioneers in the field of volunteer social work. The New York Section of the council assisted immigrant women and children, especially those traveling alone. Its president, Sadie American, wrote that many girls were "misled into immoral lives and others are subjected to great dangers because of the lack of some directing and protecting agency at Ellis Island." The council planned to be that agency.

In 1904, a woman who spoke Yiddish was hired to give assistance to unescorted women and children at Ellis Island. Eventually, the council had representatives in over two hundred fifty cities in Europe and America to help women with their immigration problems.

An investigator from NCJW visits a private home to which some immigrant girls were sent from Ellis Island.

The New York Section opened a home for unmarried women and another for Jewish girls paroled from jails or from troubled families. It had representatives to help Jewish women appearing in criminal courts. Many of these women, a council report said, "had been pushed into vice and crime by want and loneliness."

Today, the council continues to "protect and promote our social concerns through . . . community services."

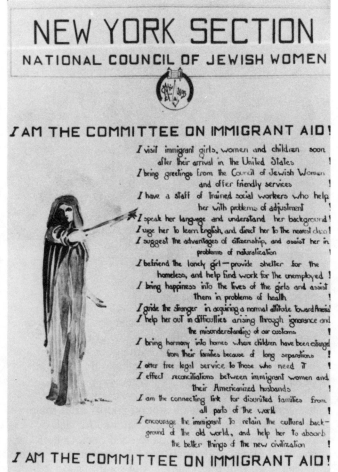

NEW YORK SECTION
NATIONAL COUNCIL OF JEWISH WOMEN

I AM THE COMMITTEE ON IMMIGRANT AID!

I visit immigrant girls, women and children soon after their arrival in the United States
I bring greetings from the Council of Jewish Women and offer friendly services
I have a staff of trained social workers who help her with problems of adjustment
I speak her language and understand her background
I urge her to learn English, and direct her to the nearest class
I suggest the advantages of citizenship, and assist her in problems of naturalization
I befriend the lonely girl — provide shelter for the homeless, and help find work for the unemployed
I bring happiness into the lives of the girls and assist them in problems of health
I guide the stranger in acquiring a normal attitude toward America
I help her out in difficulties arising through ignorance and the misunderstanding of our customs
I bring harmony into homes where children have been estranged from their families because of long separations
I offer free legal service to those who need it
I effect reconciliations between immigrant women and their Americanized husbands
I am the connecting link for disrupted families from all parts of the world
I encourage the immigrant to retain the cultural background of the old world, and help her to absorb the better things of the new civilization

I AM THE COMMITTEE ON IMMIGRANT AID!

This poem describes the aims of the Committee on Immigrant Aid of the New York Section of NCJW.

Volunteers from NCJW (far left) meet newly arrived women from Russia, about 1903.

The cemetery plot of the Skalar Benevolent Society.

Lillian Wald as a student nurse.

THE *LANDSMANSCHAFTEN*

The *landsmanschaften* were associations made up of people who came from the same town or area in Europe. Their members shared memories and perhaps homesickness for the lands and people they had left behind.

The landsmanschaften organized parties so immigrants could socialize among people from their hometowns. They also provided money for sick or needy members, raised funds to send back to their towns of origin, and purchased joint cemetery plots. It is estimated that there were about six thousand landsmanschaften in America during the height of the mass Jewish migrations.

As the native-born children of immigrants had less need of the landsmanschaften, the organizations declined. After World War II, membership increased when Holocaust survivors came to America. Today, over one thousand societies are still in existence.

LILLIAN WALD AND THE VISITING NURSES

Lillian Wald was born to a well-to-do German-Jewish family in Cincinnati in 1867, and was educated at New York Hospital's School of Nursing. In 1893, she opened a class in home nursing for Lower East Side residents. She was so horrified by the medical problems of the immigrants that she decided to live among them and help them.

Together with Mary Brewster, she founded a visiting nurse service at the Nurses' Settlement, later known as the Henry Street Settlement. By 1906, there was a staff of twenty-seven nurses working out of the settlement. They treated the immigrants' medical complaints and taught newcomers how to keep clean, healthy homes.

Wald lobbied for playgrounds, convinced city officials to hire nurses for public schools, opposed child labor, and supported workers who struck for higher wages. She also signed the "Call" that led to the founding of the National Association for the Advancement of Colored People (NAACP).

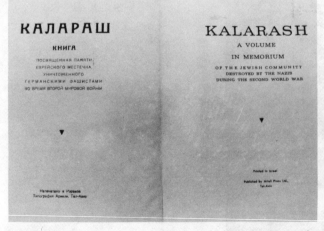

After World War II, many landsmanschaften *societies published yizkor (memorial) books in remembrance of those who died in the Holocaust. Above, the front cover of the Kalarash (U.S.S.R.) yizkor book.*

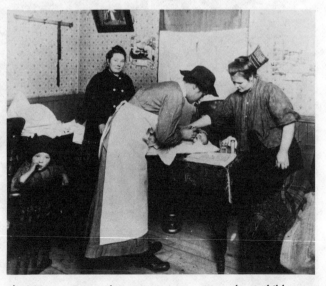

A visiting nurse teaching immigrant women about child care.

FROM OUR JEWISH HERITAGE:
The Jews as an Agricultural People

Most Jewish-Americans live in cities and have lost contact with the land. Yet from our history we learn that the Jews were originally an agricultural people.

Agriculture in the Bible

Judaism was born from an agricultural way of life. Many basic rituals of our faith are keyed to the harvest seasons in the land of Israel. Our biblical ancestors lived off the land. They raised sheep and cattle and planted crops as they were taught by God to do. (Isaiah 28:24-29)

The Bible often uses words or examples an agricultural people would understand. "He who tills his land will have plenty of bread." (Proverbs 12:11) "Your wife will be like a fruitful vine within your house; your children like olive plants around your table. So shall be blessed the man who fears the Lord." (Psalms 128:3-4) Success is measured by a full barn and vats overflowing with wine. (Proverbs 3:10)

Cultivating the land was so important to the Jews that one of the six sections of the Talmud is called *Zeraim* (Seeds). It is devoted almost entirely to agricultural questions.

Agricultural Festivals

The three major Jewish festivals—Pesaḥ, Shavuot, and Sukkot—were originally agricultural holidays. During the period of the First and Second Temples, Jews went up to Jerusalem to thank the Lord for good harvests and healthy livestock. At Pesaḥ, an *omer* (sheaf) of the first ripe barley was brought to the Temple for a ceremony that sought God's protection for the harvest. (Leviticus 23:11) For forty-nine days, from

A wall-painting from the Middle East shows how our ancestors might have harvested a field.

Pesaḥ to Shavuot, the *omer* was counted. On Shavuot, which marked the end of the barley harvest and the beginning of the wheat harvest, two loaves of bread made from the first ripe wheat were brought to the Temple as an offering of thanks. Today, homes and synagogues are decorated with fruits and flowers in remembrance of the harvest aspects of Shavuot.

Sukkot celebrated the final harvest of the year. The people were commanded to bring four types of plants—*hadar* (an etrog, a type of citrus fruit), *hadasim* (myrtle twigs), *lulav* (palm branch), and *aravot* (willows)—and "rejoice before the Lord." (Leviticus 23:40) These represented the many fruits and flowers in God's creation.

A Special Day For Trees

Another holiday related to agriculture is Tu-bi-Shevat, the "New Year of the Trees." On this holiday, fruits are eaten and Psalm 104, which praises God as the creator of all things in nature, is recited. People donate money to plant trees in the Holy Land. In Sephardic tradition, this holiday is also called the "Feast of the Fruits." At a special service in the home, blessings are said over wheat, barley, grapes, figs, pomegranates, olives, and honey. The poor are given "fruit money" (*ma'ot perot*), and children are given a *bolsa de frutas* (Judeo-Spanish for "bag of fruit").

After the Exile

When the Temple was destroyed and the years of exile began, Jews were deprived of their own land and forced to live among the other nations. Often they were forbidden to own land or to rent it for agricultural purposes. Gradually, most Jews lost contact with their agricultural heritage. The significance of the holidays as harvest festivals became less obvious to people who had never tilled the earth.

For those Jewish-Americans who live in cities, the holidays of Pesaḥ, Shavuot,

Children carrying the four types of plants for Sukkot.

A grandfather makes the blessing over bread.

Sukkot, and Tu-bi-Shevat should have special meaning. They should serve as a reminder that, in these days of computers and spaceships, we are still tied to the land for our food and that we must continually thank the Lord, *ha-motzi leḥem min ha-aretz*, "who brings forth bread from the earth."

A Brooklyn-Jewish family returns to its rural roots while vacationing in the Catskill Mountains, about 1910.

A young girl helps to harvest potatoes at an Alliance colony farm.

The prize-winning garden of a nine-year-old boy in the Alliance colony, who participated in the gardening program sponsored by the colony's benefactors.

A home decorated for Shavuot, with flowers, branches, and a picture of Moses with the Ten Commandments.

CHAPTER THREE
IMMIGRANT LIFE

Those immigrants who had expected the streets of America to be paved with gold were terribly disappointed. A character in a Yiddish novel said, "Whoever asked him, Columbus, to discover America?" Many of the immigrants would have agreed.

Poverty

A majority of the newcomers settled in large cities, especially in the eastern seaports where they had landed. They lived crowded together in tenement fire-traps with dark halls, steep stairs, and narrow windows.

Sometimes the only running water or toilets were in the hallway, shared by several families. In other cases, there was no running water at all and the toilets were outside the house.

The immigrants worked hard for low pay. Often they had to send money to help support relatives in Europe or to repay loans for their passage. It was not unusual for two or three families to live in one apartment or for a family to take in boarders to help pay the rent. In short, many immigrants found that they had exchanged the poverty of small-town Europe for the poverty of big-city America.

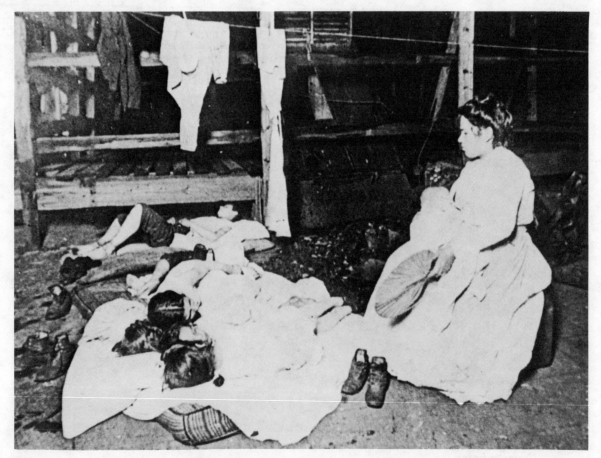

Many immigrants were very poor and lived crowded together in small rooms.

Tenements in the Jewish section of Milwaukee, about 1905.

Two views of New York's Lower East Side at the turn of the century.

The ghetto in Chicago, around 1900.

Peddler and customers on Maxwell Street, Chicago.

Some immigrants continued to wear old-fashioned clothing. Others, like the woman on the right, quickly became Americanized in their dress.

Role Changes

Newcomers to America also had to adjust to changes in the traditional ways in which members of the family related to each other. Men who were respected scholars in Europe suffered a loss of status because they could not make a living in America. Orthodox women in *sheitels* (wigs), sent for by men who had come ahead to earn money for the tickets, arrived to find that their Americanized husbands had shorn off their beards and *payot* (ritual curls). Sons who came here alone were joined by parents whose authority they rebelled against. Daughters who worked outside of the home became more independent. Children who went to public school learned English and became more American than their parents. "In America," said a Yiddish expression, "the children bring up the parents."

In the old country, a young woman usually led a sheltered life. She might work around the house until her parents arranged a marriage for her. In America, she might work in a factory, go to movies with friends, even go out on dates with men she met at work or at parties given by her landsmanschaften.

Crime

Another unpleasant fact about life in the Jewish ghettos was the level of criminal activity. Young women, lonely and friendless, were tricked into working as prostitutes. Children, left alone while their parents worked, wandered the streets and got into trouble. Some joined street gangs, others became pickpockets. In 1906, over one-third of the offenders appearing in New York's court for children were Jewish. A few of these young delinquents grew up to become notorious Jewish gangsters, such as Legs Diamond and Dopey Benny.

Single women were sometimes tricked into becoming prostitutes. This drawing by Samuel Zaget, entitled The First Step Towards a Maiden's Downfall, was printed in the Yiddish newspaper Warheit.

Families in Crisis

With little to do except stand around in the streets, children like these could get into trouble.

Sometimes a Jewish family could be broken up by the move to the New World. Husbands often went alone to America, where they tried to earn enough money to bring over the rest of their family. The long years of separation put a strain on many marriages. Some husbands just disappeared and were never heard from again. Abandoned wives looking for their husbands placed advertisements in Yiddish newspapers. Other couples were reunited only to find that they no longer wanted to live together. In 1903, Jews had the highest divorce rate of any ethnic group in New York. In the same year, 15 percent of the applications for charity in Chicago came from women deserted by their husbands. These unhappy statistics led to the establishment of a National Desertion Bureau in 1911, to help trace missing husbands.

A recurring feature in the Forward *was "A Gallery of Missing Husbands," with pictures and descriptions of men who had disappeared or deserted their wives. The first paragraph of this article is typical: "Sam Kravitz, 31 years old, was lost three and one-half years ago from Europe. He is married for five years and has one child. Eleven months ago his wife arrived and discovered that he is in St. Louis, so she went there. They lived there for three months, and seven months ago, he disappeared for a second time. He comes from Rakitnoa, Kiev [Russia], and he is a ladies' tailor by trade."*

The Good Life

Balancing this cheerless picture of the ghettos was the flourishing cultural and educational life found there and the fact that there was always the possibility of bettering oneself in America. Jews, who had been excluded from educational institutions in Europe, were eager to learn. There were public schools for children and night schools, libraries, programs at settlement houses, and technical schools for adults. By 1908, when Jews were only 2 percent of the American population, a survey of seventy-seven colleges showed that 8.5 percent of the students were first and second-generation Jews. In the 1910 graduating class of New York's City College, ninety of the one hundred twelve students were Jewish and most of these were from Eastern European families. As these numbers show, education was regarded by Jewish immigrants as the most important way to advance themselves and their children.

Above: The library of the Educational Alliance was always filled with immigrants eager to further their education. Right: Parents urged their children to study because they knew education opened the door to a better life. This drawing is by Jacob Epstein, who was born on the Lower East Side of New York in 1880, to immigrant parents from Poland. Epstein became a world-famous sculptor.

Immigrant children learned English in the public schools.

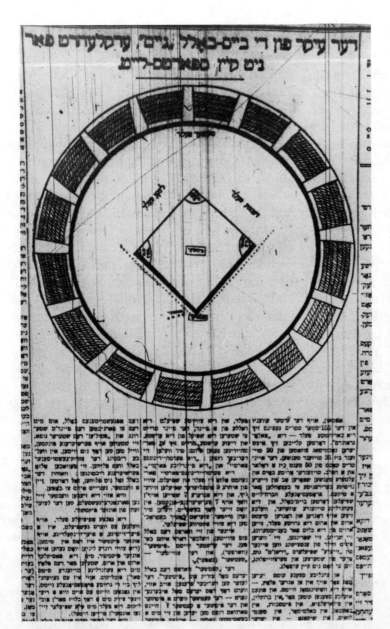

What better way to become a "real American" than to learn about baseball? In 1909, the Forward published this article, "The Rules of the Baseball 'Game' Explained for Non-Sportsmen." The article had a three-column diagram of the Polo Grounds, the old stadium of the New York Giants. It listed the baseball fields in the New York area, and gave the names of cities, towns, colleges, schools, boys clubs, and shops that organized baseball clubs. It described the layout of the baseball field, told what each player was supposed to do, and outlined the rules of scoring. The article noted that many people talked and argued about baseball, but few really knew what they were talking about.

Newspapers

The newspapers that catered to the immigrants also played an important role in educating and Americanizing them. In addition to news articles about events in this country and in the immigrants' homelands, these journals had features to teach the immigrants English and to help them adjust to life in America. Newspapers in Judeo-Spanish included *La America*, edited by Moise Gadol, and *La Vara*, edited by Albert Levy. Among the newspapers in Yiddish were the *Jewish Daily Forward*, the *Independent Wahrheit*, the *Jewish Morning Journal*, the *Chicago Daily Courier*, and the *Cleveland Jewish World*.

The most famous of these was the *Forward*, founded in 1897 and edited for almost fifty years by Abraham Cahan. One of its most appealing features was a column called *Bintel Brief* ("Bundle of Letters"), in which readers' personal problems were answered. Everyday immigrant life was reflected in the questions in this column. Is it a sin to wear face powder? Should a socialist have a religious wedding ceremony to please his parents? Is it right that a husband doesn't let his wife attend night school? The *Forward* also published stories by important Yiddish writers such as Sholom Aleichem (creator of the character Tevye in "Fiddler on the Roof") and Isaac Bashevis Singer.

Theater

Another exciting feature of immigrant life that both entertained and educated people was the theater. The Sephardim had amateur theatrical groups that produced plays in Judeo-Spanish. These were translations of French plays or original creations on biblical themes, such as "Joseph Sold By His Brothers." Typical productions based upon current events were "Dreyfus," about the French army captain victimized by anti-Semitism and "The Massacre of the Jews in Russia," about the pogroms.

The Yiddish theater was a professional enterprise with its own playhouses and stars, such as Jacob P. Adler, Boris Thomashefsky, Bertha Kalisch, and Keni Lipzin. It featured original plays inspired by current events such as the Triangle Fire, translations into Yiddish of works by classic European writers such as Tolstoy, Gorky, Goethe, and Ibsen, as well as Jewish versions of Shakespeare's plays. In "Romeo and Juliet," the Christian Friar Lawrence became a Reform rabbi. In *"Der Yiddisher Kenig Lir"* ("The Jewish King Lear"), Shakespeare's English ruler became a Russian Jew who, like Lear, had trouble with his three daughters. Immigrants could understand this conflict between generations, which reminded them of their own problems with their Americanized children.

At the height of its glory, Yiddish theater attracted between five and seven thousand people each night in New York. Appreciative audiences went to the Standard and National theaters in Philadelphia, Glickman's in Chicago, and productions in other cities starring actors on tour or local players.

Sephardic and Yiddish theater and newspapers declined in popularity as the children of immigrants learned English.

Amateur groups also produced plays in the various languages spoken by Jewish immigrants. In 1929, the Israelite Philanthropic Organization sponsored this production of Shakespeare's Romeo and Juliet *in Arabic.*

The noted Yiddish actress Bertha Kalisch.

A theater poster advertising Jacob Adler as King Lear.

A drawing by Jacob Epstein of the audience at a Yiddish theater production.

Crowds awaiting entrance to the Grand Theater on the Lower East Side, about 1904.

Boris Thomashefsky as Hamlet.

Religious Life

For some immigrants, becoming an American meant becoming less religious. The story is told of one young man who stood at the railing of the boat that brought him to America and threw his *tefilin* (ritual prayer articles) into the sea.

Most of the immigrants remained orthodox, however, and the synagogue was the center of their lives. If they could not afford to build a synagogue, they prayed in rented stores or tenement rooms. Immigrant societies held their own services so people from the same hometowns could pray in ways familiar to them.

Religious schools were opened. They were generally underfunded and staffed by low-quality teachers. The immigrants often found that their children preferred to be educated in public schools and to pray with Conservative or Reform congregations, which they believed were more American and more modern than the schools and synagogues of their parents.

Rosh Hashanah worshipers outside a tenement synagogue on Rivington Street in New York, about 1910.

A Jewish boy on the day of his bar mitzvah (1920).

This synagogue at 280 Broome Street on the Lower East Side was built by Jews from Ioannina, Greece. Although they used Sephardic ritual, they were not actually Sephardim. They were Greek-speaking Jews whose ancestors had lived in Ioannina as early as the ninth century.

The parade marking the opening of the Syrian school Magen David Talmud Torah, in Brooklyn, 1926.

The Syrians

Among the immigrants was a group of Arabic-speaking Jews from Syria who settled in New York. Their adjustment to America was doubly difficult. They felt uncomfortable in Ashkenazi synagogues where the congregants chatted in Yiddish and sang unfamiliar melodies with a different Hebrew pronunciation. They were equally ill at ease among the assimilated, established Sephardim at Shearith Israel and the Judeo-Spanish speaking immigrants from Greece and Turkey. They went to kosher restaurants to eat and were confronted by unfamiliar European dishes such as blintzes, gefilte fish, and chopped liver, so different from the Arabic food they knew.

As a result, the Syrian Jews were very clannish. They had their own synagogue and school. They worked together, usually as peddlars or in cigar factories. They married other Syrians and socialized at their own café on the corner of Allen and Grand Streets on the Lower East Side. As they prospered, they moved to Brooklyn where, today, there exists a community of descendants of these pioneer Syrian immigrants.

A haggadah in Hebrew and Arabic, used by Jews from Arab lands who came to America. This page illustrates the plagues of darkness and slaying of the first-born.

CLOSE-UPS: *Immigrant Life*

Abraham Saron and his ten children.

Jacob Greenblatt taking chickens to the railroad station for delivery to Philadelphia.

IMMIGRANT TINSMITHS, CARPENTERS, DANCERS, AND ICE SKATERS

The first of the Saron children to come to America was David, the oldest son. He arrived in 1885 and worked as a tinsmith so that he could send money to his family in Shavel, Lithuania. His brother Jacob followed within the year. Jacob's first job in America was participating in the final assembly of the Statue of Liberty. He also worked on the copper roofs of the buildings at Columbia University.

Between 1886 and 1891, five more of the Saron children came to America. Abraham Saron, their father, remained in Shavel, where he studied Torah and Jewish law and his wife ran an inn. He had no head for business, and when she died, the inn soon failed. In 1891, Abraham and his two youngest children came to America. The last of the Sarons to arrive was Libby, whose husband sent her money to join him in Chicago in 1892.

Abraham's daughter Mollie studied dance with the father of silent-screen star Theda Bara. Her brothers Wolf and Victor were carpenters and housepainters. Victor later became a professional ice skater and for several years, he taught skating to members of the British royal family who were vacationing in Canada.

LIFE IN THE ALLIANCE COLONY

With the help of the Baron de Hirsch Fund, Jacob Greenblatt left Kovel, Russia, in 1890. Two years later he had earned enough money to send steerage tickets to his wife, Golda, and their children. The family lived in Brotmanville, New Jersey, part of the Jewish farming community of Alliance. Trained as a carpenter, Jacob helped build houses in the town. When this was done, he took a loan from the fund to build a small shop and barn, and became a butcher.

The Greenblatts kept horses for transportation and cows for cheese, milk, and butter. Their son Joseph had a prize-winning vegetable garden that supplied fresh greens in summer and root vegetables that were stored for winter use. He and the other children were excused from school during the harvest season, and with their mother, supplemented the family income by working on nearby farms. They harvested peas, beans, and sweet potatoes. They picked cranberries from the bogs. They also worked in a tomato canning factory.

This orthodox family felt lucky when the community decided to found its own synagogue, which Jacob helped build. The synagogue became the focus of Jewish life in Brotmanville. On many a Shabbat, Golda and her daughters sat in the women's curtained balcony and listened to Jacob read from the Torah.

Victor Saron skating with Princess Patricia, granddaughter of Britain's Queen Victoria.

B'nai Moshe Anshe Astreich Congregation, the synagogue that Jacob helped build.

Pauline Cohen and Adolf Schwartz

Marco and Sultana Romey with five of their children.

AN "UPTOWN" JEW MARRIES AN IMMIGRANT

Pauline Cohen's grandparents were part of the wave of German Jews who came to America in the late 1840s. She was born in New York, and raised and educated in Richmond, Virginia. The immigrants referred to a native-born Jew like Pauline as "a real Yankee."

In 1902, Pauline was introduced to Adolf Schwartz. He had been employed as a dancing teacher, a steel-worker and a butcher. Although Hungarian-born, he had come to this country at the age of ten and spoke English without an accent. But to Pauline, he would always be "a foreigner." She married him because he was handsome, bright, and charming, but she made him change his "foreign-sounding name" to Edward.

Pauline and Edward named their children Cecilia, William, and Melvin. Pauline always said that she decided against the name "Morris" for her third child because it wasn't "fancy enough." The family lived in Harlem, New York City, then a Jewish neighborhood.

Melvin Schwartz in Harlem.

SEPHARDIM IN SEATTLE

In the early 1900s, Marco Romey and Sultana Policar came to this country to escape the poverty of their native Turkey. They met and married in Seattle, where each had come to join the community of Sephardim from Turkey and Rhodes. Marco worked on the docks, loading ships. He decided the work was too strenuous,

so he went to night school and became licensed as a barber.

Fiercely proud of their Sephardic heritage, the Romeys and their seven children spoke Judeo-Spanish at home. The children acted in the local amateur productions of the Sephardic theater. Marco subscribed to *La America* and *La Vara*. When the newspapers arrived in the mail, the family gathered around while he read stories aloud. If there was news of famine or floods in Turkey, Marco helped raise funds for the Jewish communities there.

The Romeys were orthodox Jews who closed their barbershop on Shabbat. Marco was president of the Sephardic Bikur Holim Synagogue. His grandson, Marc Angel, became rabbi of Shearith Israel, the Spanish-Portuguese synagogue in New York.

La America, a Judeo-Spanish newspaper widely read by Sephardic immigrants.

Yusif Rishty and his daughter Gilsum.

FROM ALEPPO TO NEW YORK

Yusif and Mazal Rishty and their five children lived in Aleppo, Syria. Yusif had horses and buggies which he used to transport people between the towns of Syria. But the economy of Aleppo declined, and in 1910 Yusif left his family and went to America to seek his fortune.

Yusif stayed with a Syrian family on the Lower East Side of New York. He made a living peddling dry goods. He and his fellow immigrants from Syria prayed together in a rented room over a store. In his spare time, Yusif played *tówleh* (backgammon) at a Syrian cafe.

By 1911, Yusif had enough money to go to Syria for his wife and four younger children, whom he brought to America. His oldest son, Ezra, had gone to Argentina in 1910 to avoid being drafted. Now he joined the family in New York. The Rishtys Americanized their names: Yusif became Joseph, Mazal became Mollie, Jemal became James, and Zarefa became Sophie. But they preserved their Syrian heritage by speaking Arabic at home, listening to Arabic music, and eating the rice and stuffed vegetable dishes of their native land.

In 1926, the family was living in Brooklyn, where Yusif and Mazal's grandchildren are part of the vibrant Syrian-Jewish community today.

SMALL-TOWN JEWISH LIFE

Morris Lass came to this country from Russia in 1883. He boarded with a Levine family and took their name. When he had earned enough money, he brought his wife Mary and their children to America.

The Levines went to Kingston, in upstate New York, where other Jews from their Russian town had settled. Morris and most of these immigrants were peddlars. They traveled around the Hudson Valley countryside for a month at a time carrying their goods in packs on their backs, or, if they were lucky, in a horse and wagon. They sold clothing and tin pots, or traded for junk, fur pelts, and fruits from local orchards, which they shipped back to Kingston.

Morris and Mary had three grown daughters, who, the parents felt, were not meeting enough eligible Jewish men. So in 1906, the family moved to Brooklyn. The Levines' oldest son, Benjamin, had married a local Jewish woman and his descendants still live in the Kingston area.

Benjamin Levine (far right) and his partners in the Kingston Fur and Junk Company.

The Goldfarbs' store in Elk Rapids, around 1900.

Tibbie Goldfarb

Aaron Goldfarb

team. Aaron was an educated man who spoke five languages and learned Chippewa to communicate with his Indian customers.

Tibbie was a religious woman who wore a *sheitel* (wig) and kept a strictly kosher home. She bought meat from Traverse City, a town seventeen miles away that had about forty Jewish families, a *shoḥet* (kosher butcher) and a synagogue. On holidays, the Goldfarbs attended services in Traverse City, and once a month Tibbie traveled there by horse and buggy or sleigh to go to the *mikveh* (ritual bathhouse).

In many of the small towns of northern Michigan there was a single Jewish family which ran a dry-goods store. Although geographically separated, the Jewish community was unified. They all bought goods from the same salesman from Detroit, met at Traverse City's synagogue, and frequently got together for family celebrations.

A HARD-WORKING IMMIGRANT HELPS BUILD AMERICA

Charles Taratotsky was a skilled bricklayer from Bialystok, Russia. When he came to America at the beginning of the twentieth century, his brother-in-law Abraham Friedberg arranged for him to join the Bricklayer's Union.

"What's your name?" the union official asked when Charles went to join. Charles did not understand English and thought the man had asked, "Who sent you?" "Abraham Friedberg," he replied. It was under that name that Charles was enrolled in the union, and by that name he became known.

To save the fare, Charles always walked to job sites.

THE ONLY JEWS IN TOWN

Aaron Goldfarb arrived in the U.S. from Zhitomir, Russia, around 1880. He went to northern Michigan to work as a lumberjack. After he injured his foot, he became a pack peddlar. By 1893, he and his wife Tibbie had opened a dry-goods store in Elk Rapids, a small town that was little more than a shopping center for the surrounding lumber camps.

The Goldfarbs had seven children and a sign in the store window which said, "We grow our own clerks." Aaron would leave their children in charge of the store while he went fishing or watched the local baseball

Charles "Abraham Friedberg" Taratotsky (left) and his brother-in-law Abraham Friedberg.

Jacob Weisenthal with his daughter Ethel.

According to union rules, a man did not have to lay more than a certain number of bricks per day. Charles insisted on doing as many as he could, so the bosses always gave him the hardest jobs: laying brick around windows and corners. A tireless worker, Charles did not retire until his seventies, after he fell from a scaffold.

Charles never joined a *landsmanschaften* because he was so happy to be in America that he didn't want to associate with "the old country." In the East Broadway apartment where they raised their ten children, Charles and his wife, Rose, always hung an American flag and a picture of the nation's president.

Charles helped lay the bricks for the front of the Bialystok Home for the Aged, which still stands on East Broadway in New York.

A "GREENHORN" LEAVES THE SWEATSHOP

In 1909, Galician-born Jacob Weisenthal paid ten dollars to the owner of a clothing factory for the privilege of learning how to sew the waists on men's knickers. While he learned, Jake was paid no salary. Then he received twenty-five cents for every dozen pairs of pants he sewed. The problem was that the manager of the factory gave small-sized pants to his family and friends. To the "greenhorn," which is what new immigrants were sometimes called, he gave size

eighteens. It took longer to make the waists on these big pants, so Jake only earned between $1.50 and $2.00 per week. Out of this, he gave fifty cents each week to the union, until his five-dollar dues were paid.

When the union called a strike, the owner agreed to settle only if "that slow greener" was fired. Jake explained to the union man about the manager's favoritism in giving out sizes. The union threatened to continue the strike unless the "greener" was rehired. In a compromise, the owner agreed to give Jake back the ten-dollar learner's fee. Fed up with the garment industry, Jake went to work for a cousin in the egg business. He founded his own egg company and became a member of the New York Mercantile Exchange.

Jake met Ida Einbinder, who worked in a ladies' blouse factory, at a dance given by his *landsmanschaften*. They married and their American-born children, Ethel and Martin, spoke only Yiddish until they learned English in public school.

Ida Einbinder at Coney Island.

HOMESTEADERS IN NORTH DAKOTA

When Russian-born Solomon Dellar and his children landed in Philadelphia, they were destined for the American West. Solomon had no experience as a farmer—in Odessa, he had manufactured talcum powder—but the family was going to try rural life in America.

The Dellars went to Painted Woods, North Dakota, where the Baron de Hirsch Fund had organized a Jewish agricultural settlement. According to the Homestead Act, if a person lived on this land for five years and improved it by farming, it would belong to him after payment of a ten-dollar fee.

Although his sons John and Joseph soon left North Dakota, Solomon, his son Levy, and daughter Esther, were determined to succeed. They cleared the land and planted barley and wheat. They worked hard, but nature was against them. There were blizzards in winter, too much rain, and droughts during the growing season.

The colony at Painted Woods failed, but the Dellars managed to stay on the land for five years. They sold their homestead and moved to Oregon, where they tried farming but again were unsuccessful. Recognizing that they were not meant to be farmers, the Dellars settled in Portland and went into the clothing and shoe business.

Solomon Dellar

Esther Dellar

Drawings by S. Levy of the Jewish agricultural settlement in North Dakota.

The immigrants' world (starting from top left): a street scene in the ghetto. Top right: An Epstein drawing of a father and son going to shul. Middle left: An old man with a Yiddish newspaper. Middle center: Immigrant women selling eggs. Middle right: Children of immigrants wearing Brooklyn Dodger baseball uniforms. Bottom: A demonstration for higher wages.

CHAPTER FOUR
THE RISE OF THE UNIONS

Tea and Politics

In the cafés of the Jewish ghettos in the United States, lively groups of intellectuals sat over cups of tea arguing politics. Many of them were socialists who had organized workers in Europe. As socialists, they believed that the government should own all means of production and distribution of essential goods, and that people should be provided with their basic needs, such as food, clothing, and shelter. They felt that public ownership was preferable to private enterprise based upon competition, and they denounced "capitalist bosses" who took advantage of the workers. They urged the Jewish immigrants to unionize and to fight for improvements in their working conditions.

Jewish Reaction to the Unions

In 1888, the United Hebrew Trades was formed, to unionize Jewish workers. Other unions with large Jewish memberships included the International Ladies Garment Workers Union (ILGWU), the Amalgamated Clothing Workers Union, the Cap Makers Union, and the Fur Workers Union. These had only limited success. Many Jews saw themselves as temporary employees. Men hoped to be owners someday; women dreamt of quitting when they married. Many of the orthodox distrusted the socialists, whom they regarded as atheists. The workers were less interested in politics than in survival. They worked hard to support their families, to earn enough money to open their own businesses, or to bring relatives over from Europe.

To others, the disruption of the family and the confusion about new roles and about the place of religion in life, had left them with a spiritual void which the socialists rushed to fill. Their poverty made the socialists' vi-

A café scene drawn by Jacob Epstein.

Women on strike selling socialist newspapers.

sion appealing. For these people, socialism replaced Judaism, and the union hall, rather than the synagogue, became the focus of their lives.

Working Conditions

The labor organizers made great progress in the garment industry, where large numbers of Jewish immigrants were employed. Garment workers slaved long hours for low pay. They worked under dreadful conditions, in factories that were disease-ridden firetraps with poor ventilation. There were also tenement sweatshops where people were paid according to the number of pieces they sewed. They had to supply their own sewing machines, needles, and thread, and pay for their own electricity. The garment workers were miserable, but they did not have the power to change their terrible conditions. They realized that labor unions could give them that power and help them improve their lives.

The factories and sweatshops of the early twentieth century.

The Uprising of the Twenty Thousand

Conditions were particularly bad in the shirtwaist (ladies' blouse) industry. The workers, mostly young Jewish and Italian women, set up picket lines at two shops, the Triangle Waist Company and Lieserson's. On November 22, 1909, the workers called a meeting in the Cooper Union building to discuss whether or not to go on strike. After several hours of debate, a young woman asked to speak. Her name was Clara Lemlich and she had spent days on the picket line at Lieserson's.

I am a working girl, one of those striking against intolerable conditions. I am tired of listening to speakers who talk in generalities. What we are here for is to decide whether or not to strike. I offer a resolution that a general strike be declared—now! [Louis Levine, *The Women's Garment Workers*]

There was wild cheering for five minutes after her challenge. The motion was seconded and the chairman asked the audience, "Do you mean it in good faith? Will you take the old Jewish oath?" Thousands of workers raised their hands. "If I turn traitor to the cause I now pledge," they said, echoing the words of Psalm 137:5, "may this hand wither from the arm I raise."

Teenage activist Clara Lemlich was described as a "pint of trouble for the bosses."

This painting of scenes from the shirtwaist makers' strike is by the artist Philip Reisman. In the middle, with her hand raised, is Clara Lemlich at the Cooper Union meeting.

The strike that began so dramatically came to be called "The Uprising of the Twenty Thousand." Within the next month, over seven hundred workers were arrested. Public sympathy was with the strikers and on February 10, 1910, the strike was settled. The International Ladies Garment Workers Union (ILGWU) gained in strength. Although it did not get recognition from the employers, it achieved some improvements in working conditions.

Highlights of a Shirtwaist Maker's Day —Scribne

She finds time to take her turn on the picket line.

At a shop meeting, Business Agent Minnie Rosen tells what must be done.

On the street, she frowns at a scab.

With her working sisters in the pressing department she stages a sit-down strike to support the demands of the cutters.

In the evening she listens to speakers, in the great hall at Cooper Union, explain the necessity for united action.

Police taking striking shirtwaist makers to the Jefferson Market prison.

A contemporary newspaper drawing of how a shirtwaist maker might spend her day during the strike.

"Going out for better conditions" was the caption the photographer gave this picture of women on strike, 1909.

The Great Revolt

In July 1910, another strike began, a well-planned walk-out by over sixty thousand workers in the cloak industry. This strike, which became known as "The Great Revolt," brought production to a halt. Most of the workers, strike leaders, and employers were Jewish. During the next three months, there was much violence and bad publicity for the Jewish community, which greatly disturbed the uptown Jews. Louis Marshall, Jacob Schiff, and numerous rabbis and social workers tried to mediate between labor and management.

The 1910 strike ended with the "Protocol of Peace," an agreement engineered by Louis Brandeis, a Boston attorney who had helped to settle a recent garment industry strike in that city. The Protocol provided for a permanent arbitration board to handle labor disputes and a Joint Board of Sanitary Control to improve working conditions in the industry.

A rally of cloakmakers on strike.

Louis Brandeis, who later was the first Jew appointed to the bench of the Supreme Court of the United States.

"In unity is our strength."

The Triangle Fire

Public attention was drawn again to New York's garment district on March 25, 1911, when a fire broke out in the factory of the Triangle Waist Company. Within minutes, the fire flashed through the company's three floors. Workers were trapped behind doors that were locked because the owners were concerned about theft by employees. In a supposedly fireproof building, one hundred forty-six workers died and many others were injured. Most of the dead were young Jewish and Italian women who had been suffocated by smoke, engulfed by flames, or had jumped to their deaths in vain efforts to escape the inferno behind them. Many of these women had participated in the Revolt of the Twenty Thousand, when they had demanded safer working conditions. As a newspaper reporter wrote, their "dead bodies were the answer."

"The Morgue is Filled With Our Sacrifices," the *Forward*'s headline read the next day. "The Whole Jewish Community [Is] In Mourning." Public opinion was aroused by the fire, which resulted in sympathy for the union movement, and ultimately, the passage of laws to improve working conditions.

Top: A newspaper printed this drawing of Triangle workers jumping to their deaths. Middle: The remains of the Triangle factory after the fire. Left: The funeral procession honoring victims of the Triangle disaster. Above right: A call in English, Yiddish, and Italian to attend the memorial for the Triangle victims.

The Chicago Strike of 1910

In other cities, such as Boston, Cleveland, Philadelphia, Chicago, and Baltimore, there were also strikes and attempts to unionize Jewish workers. For the most part, these labor actions were not as successful as they were in New York. A notable exception was the historic strike in Chicago that began on September 22, 1910, when a group of young women walked off their jobs at Hart, Schaffner & Marx, the city's largest men's garment manufacturer. They were protesting a cut in their pay for seaming pants, from 4¢ to 3¾¢ per piece. By mid-October, most of their 8,000 co-workers had followed them, and eventually, 38,000 people throughout the men's clothing industry in Chicago went out on strike.

After a bitter four-month struggle during which two workers were killed, the strike brought few appreciable gains to most of Chicago's workers. However, an important settlement was reached at Hart, Schaffner & Marx. The contract provided that all striking employees of the company would be rehired and that there would be no discrimination against workers based on union membership. It also established an Arbitration Committee to consider workers' complaints.

Top: Four of the young women who walked off their jobs during the 1910 strike in Chicago.

Middle: A parade of workers during the Chicago strike, 1910.

Bottom: Passions were strong on each side and strikes often got violent.

A newsboy announces the settlement at Hart, Schaffner & Marx.

Arbitration

The New York "Protocol of Peace" and the Chicago agreement for arbitration, or negotiation, signified a new era in labor-management relations. It has been suggested that this breakthrough came because many of the employers and employees involved in the garment industry strikes were Jews and were receptive to the idea of arbitration because it was a familiar part of their heritage. When the Jewish nation was conquered, Jews became governed by non-Jewish law and non-Jewish courts that often discriminated against them. To preserve the Jewish legal system, parties often agreed to have their claims settled by arbitration within the Jewish community. Arbitration as a method of resolving disputes between employers and employees may well be the most important contribution that the Jewish labor movement made to American trade unionism.

A woman testifies before the Trade Board at Hart, Schaffner & Marx, made up of representatives from the union and the firm.

Strikes and strikers (starting from top left): A strike of clothing workers in St. Louis, 1912. Top right: This poster memorializes a young woman killed during the strike of garment workers in Rochester, New York, in 1913. Left: October 1915, Chicago: 15,000 garment workers on strike. Bottom left: Raising provisions for striking tailors. Bottom right: Workers selling the newspapers that support their strike.

CLOSE-UPS: *Jews and the Labor Movement*

Morris Hillquit

A SOCIALIST LEADER

Latvian-born Morris Hillquit emigrated to America in 1886. A dedicated socialist, he became a noted figure in the political life of the Lower East Side.

Although Russian was his native tongue, Hillquit learned to speak Yiddish in America so he could communicate with the Jewish workers. He felt it was important to educate them culturally so they could develop an "intelligent understanding of their own problems" and an interest in the class struggle. He taught English to the immigrants in night school and helped found the *Arbeiter-Zeitung* "Workers' Paper," which was concerned with both socialist and general cultural issues.

Hillquit was the first secretary of the United Hebrew Trades. In this early stage of the Jewish labor movement, Hillquit thought the Jews were "unorganizable." They were interested in the unions only when there was a strike and that interest died with the end of the strikes. It was only after the 1910 strikes, he later wrote, that the Jewish worker understood the importance of the unions.

Hillquit graduated from New York University Law School, and became a leading member of the Socialist Party of America. He ran for Congress, and in 1917 was a candidate for mayor of New York.

AN EMPLOYER WITH A CONSCIENCE

Joseph Schaffner was born in Reedsburg, Ohio to German-Jewish parents. He became a founder of Hart, Schaffner & Marx, the biggest garment manufacturer in Chicago. His contemporaries described him as "sensitive, with a sort of conscience that led to much reflection and constant questioning of self."

Involved with the management and promotion end of the business, Schaffner was not aware of conditions in the factories. The 1910 strike came as a surprise to him. He was crushed by the criticism of rabbis and social workers and began to wonder whether he was "a moral failure" in life.

After a striking worker was shot to death, Schaffner took over the labor negotiations from his associates. He soon realized that the heart of the problem was the workers' need to have a way to express complaints. The historic Hart, Schaffner & Marx agreement setting up an arbitration committee was in large measure due to Schaffner's intervention.

Joseph Schaffner once said:

It is useless for us to say that we are not striving to make money because it is the measure, after all, of success; but it is gratifying at the same time to feel that it is coupled with an ethical principle that puts us on a big, broad, moral foundation. The best evidence of this is that people generally acknowledge we have done much to raise the standard of the clothing industry. [*Joseph Schaffner: Recollections and Impressions of His Associates*]

Schaffner's contribution was recognized by the Amalgamated Clothing Workers Union which named him among the "Chicago Friends of the Amalgamated."

Joseph Schaffner

SAMUEL GOMPERS, PRESIDENT OF THE AFL

Samuel Gompers came to America from London with his Dutch-Jewish parents in 1863. A cigarmaker like his father, he joined the Cigarmakers International Union. In 1886, he helped to organize the American Federation of Labor (AFL) and was its president until his death in 1924.

Gompers differed greatly from many of the other Jews in the labor movement. He strongly opposed socialism. He believed that politics had no place in the union movement. He even wanted to restrict immigration to protect jobs for the American worker. This policy upset many Jewish immigrants who wanted to bring their relatives to America.

At first, Gompers objected to the formation of separate unions for Jews. "In the labor movement," he said, "we are not Jews nor Christians nor atheists, but we are working men bound by the common ties." Gompers later decided that Jewish unions were a first step in bringing Jews into the mainstream of American labor. He supported the attempts to organize the garment workers and was a featured speaker at many of their strike rallies. He appeared at the famous 1909 meeting of Cooper Union that led to the shirtwaist makers' strike.

Top: Samuel Gompers

Middle: The seal of the American Federation of Labor showed clasped hands, a symbol of trade union solidarity. The seal was said to be based on the emblem of the Sephardi self-help society, Hand-in-Hand, of which Gompers and his parents were members.

Bottom: Samuel Gompers addressing a meeting of 3,000 shirtwaist makers at Cooper Union, 1909.

Rose Schneiderman

A WOMAN RISES THROUGH THE RANKS

Rose Schneiderman and her family came to New York from Saven, Russian-Poland, in 1890. At their first Pesaḥ seder in America, she later wrote, they had "a sense of safety and hope that we had never felt in Poland."

When she was sixteen, Schneiderman took a job in a hat factory. In 1903, she was elected secretary of Local 23 of the United Cloth Hat and Cap Makers Union. Within a year, she was a member of the union's General Executive Board, the first woman to hold a high position in the labor movement.

In 1905, Schneiderman joined the Women's Trade Union League, which was dedicated to helping women workers organize and better their conditions. After the Triangle Fire she addressed a memorial meeting for its victims:

Schneiderman (center) in the office of the Women's Trade Union League during the 1909 shirtwaist makers' strike.

This is not the first time girls have been burned alive in this city. Every week I must learn of the untimely death of one of my sister workers. Every year thousands of us are maimed. The life of men and women is so cheap and property is so sacred! [Lucy Goldthwaite and Rose Schneiderman, *All for One*]

Schneiderman devoted her life to the labor movement. She was an organizer for the ILGWU and the White Goods Workers Union and served for many years as president of the Women's Trade Union League.

Jacob Epstein's drawing of Morris Rosenfeld. Behind the poet is a sweatshop worker, "toiling without let-up in that sunless den."

A SWEATSHOP POET

Morris Rosenfeld was born in the small town of Bolkshein in Russian-Poland, and came to New York in 1886. He made a poor living working as a presser in a sweatshop, and at night he worked on his poems.

Rosenfeld became known as the "Poet Laureate of Labor," and wrote in Yiddish. In his poem, "The Sweatshop," he described the life of sweatshop workers:

Toiling without letup in that sunless den:
nimble-fingered and (or so it seems) content,
sit some thirty blighted women, blighted men,
with their spirits broken and their bodies spent.

In *Mayn Yingele* ("My Little Boy"), Rosenfeld wrote sorrowfully of his child, who was asleep when he left for work and asleep again when he returned late at night:

. . . seldom do I see him when
he's wide awake and bright. . . .
The time-clock drags me off at dawn;
at night it lets me go,
I hardly know my flesh and blood;
his eyes I hardly know.

[Irving Howe and Kenneth Libo, *How We Lived*]

CAHAN, THE *FORWARD*, AND JEWISH LABOR

On August 19, 1882, Abraham Cahan made a two-hour speech in Yiddish. In simple terms, he explained the theory of socialism to an audience of Jewish immigrants. Until that time, most of the leaders of the Jewish labor movement were Russian-speaking intellectuals who did not understand that they could best reach their fellow immigrants by talking in Yiddish.

Cahan had arrived in New York two months earlier from Pabrade, Lithuania. A natural teacher, he spoke of socialism in terms that uneducated Jewish immigrants could understand. He compared the coming of the Messiah with the approaching socialist revolution, and compared Israel's liberation from Egyptian bondage with the socialist liberation of workers from exploiting bosses.

Cahan was one of the founders of the United Hebrew Trades, but it was as editor of the *Jewish Daily Forward* that he made his greatest mark. Under his guidance, the *Forward* educated and Americanized the immigrants, and was a powerful voice of the labor movement. During a strike by bakers, for example, the *Forward* appealed to Jews as a community:

> It is wholly a domestic matter with us. The workmen are ours and the bosses are ours. . . . Let us show the world that when a struggle like this occurs in our midst, we settle the question in a feeling of justice and human sympathy—that we settle the issue in favor of the workmen and their just demands. [Moses Rischin, *The Promised City*]

Cahan served as the *Forward*'s editor from 1902 until his death in 1951.

Newsboys in front of the Forward *building on the Lower East Side.*

Abraham Cahan.

THE WORKING WOMAN'S NOVELIST

Soon after sixteen-year-old Anzia Yezierska arrived in New York, she got a job working in a sweatshop. She went to work before dawn and left after sunset, spending her day sewing buttons on clothing. She wrote in her autobiography:

> I didn't have a room to myself, even a bed. I slept on a mattress on the floor in a rathole of a room occupied by a dozen other immigrants. I was always hungry—oh, so hungry! The scant meals I could hardly afford only sharpened my appetite for real food. [Anzia Yezierska, *Red Ribbon on a White Horse*]

Her employer, who she said "looked like a black witch," seemed in her eyes to become "a huge greedy maw for wanting more and more buttons." When her boss insisted that she work even longer hours, Yezierska refused and was fired. "I want no clock watcher in my shop," her employer said. "Out you go!"

Yezierska worked as a waitress, a cook, and a teacher before becoming a successful writer. She was known as "The Historian of Hester Street," and her realistic stories about immigrant life were drawn from her own experiences. Among her books are *Hungry Hearts,* which was made into a Hollywood movie, *Salome of the Tenements*, and *Bread Givers*.

Sidney Hillman

Anzia Yezierska

Later, Hillman was influential in Democratic party politics and was an adviser to President Franklin Roosevelt. "Clear it with Sidney," was Roosevelt's predictable response to questions relating to labor. A vice-president of the World Federation of Trade Unions, Hillman was also interested in the Jewish labor movement in Palestine and tried to persuade Roosevelt to adopt a more pro-Zionist position.

FROM RABBINICAL STUDENT TO UNION PRESIDENT

Sidney Hillman, the grandson of a rabbi, was a student at a rabbinical seminary in Kovno, Lithuania, when he rebelled against his traditional upbringing and became a labor organizer. In 1905, he was jailed because of his political activities. After his release, he came to America and settled in Chicago.

During the 1910 strike begun by workers at Hart, Schaffner & Marx, the deep-voiced young Hillman emerged as a leader. He was quick-witted and had an analytical mind, which one of his biographers attributed to his Talmudic training. He believed in moderation and viewed the strike settlement as an implied recognition of the union by the manufacturers.

In 1914, Hillman became president of the Amalgamated Clothing Workers. Within a year, the union was the chief bargaining agent for the men's garment industry. By 1918, the union had won a forty-four hour work week. Two years later, the employers agreed to a contract that guaranteed unemployment insurance. They also agreed to employ only members of the union.

Hillman (left) with Frank Rosenblum, a Chicago garment worker who was fired because of his union activities.

FROM OUR JEWISH HERITAGE:
The Laborer

Jews are but a small percentage of the total American population, yet a large number of the leaders of labor unions have been Jewish. What is there in our Jewish heritage that might explain Jewish activism in the labor movement?

The Blessing of Work

In some ancient cultures, such as the Greek and Roman, labor was considered degrading. This has never been the Jewish view. Jews have considered labor a blessing given by God. The job of the first human being, Adam, was to till and guard the Garden of Eden. (Genesis 2:15) "Great is work," says the Talmud, "for it honors those who do it."

Throughout the Bible, the worker is glorified. The man who "is skilled in his work" is praised (Proverbs 22:29), as is the woman who "works with willing hands." (Proverbs 31:13)

The Work Cycle

The very first sentence of the Bible praises God as the world's foremost worker, who created the heavens and the earth. The opening chapters of Genesis read like a work-log, describing in detail how God labored for six days and then rested on the seventh. Following the pattern set by the Lord, the people of Israel were commanded to work for six days and then to rest on the Sabbath. (Exodus 20:9-10) *Havdalah*, the ceremony marking the end of the Sabbath, blesses the Lord for making "a distinction . . . between the seventh day and the six working days. . . ." It is after a hard week's labor and through the withdrawal from everyday work and cares that one appreciates the physical and spiritual rest of a traditional Shabbat.

"Rachel came with her father's sheep, for she tended them." (Genesis 29:10)

Jacob and Laban

Jewish law has always been concerned about employers exploiting employees. This was a problem even in ancient times. Was not the story of Laban and his nephew Jacob actually about a biblical employer who took advantage of a worker? Before Jacob began to serve Laban, he and his uncle agreed upon the length of his contract and the amount of his pay: Jacob was to work for seven years in return for the hand of Laban's daughter Rachel. At the end of seven years, Laban defrauded Jacob out of his "salary" by tricking him into marrying Rachel's sister Leah. Jacob had to work for Laban another seven years before Laban fulfilled the original contract and allowed Jacob to marry Rachel. (Genesis 29: 15-28)

Jacob with Rachel, Leah, and Laban.

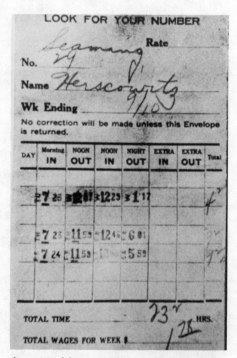

A pay-card for a garment worker in the early part of this century. The worker received $1.78 for more than 23 hours of work.

Employer and Employee

There are numerous guidelines about how an employer should treat those whom he hires. For example, the Torah commands that a laborer should be paid his wages on the same day he earns them. (Deuteronomy 24:15; Leviticus 19:13) This law recognizes that many workers are poor and need their money each day in order to eat. The failure of employers to pay on time is often denounced by the prophets. Malachi condemns those "who oppress the hireling in his wages." (Malachi 3:5) Jeremiah preaches against the person "who makes his fellow-man work without pay and does not give him his wages." (Jeremiah 22:13)

The recognition of the dignity of work and the needs of the laborer are an essential part of the Jewish tradition. It is therefore not surprising that so many Jews were prominent participants in the formation of American labor unions.

Top left: Bessie Abramowitz led the women who walked off the job at Hart, Schaffner & Marx in 1910. She married Sidney Hillman, whom she met during the strike. After his death in 1946, she became a vice-president of the Amalgamated Clothing and Textile Workers Union.

Top right: Garment-worker Pauline Newman became a union organizer during the 1909 strike. She devoted her life to the ILGWU and spent more than sixty years as educational director of its Union Health Center.

Left: David Dubinsky was president of the ILGWU, one of the nation's largest unions, from 1932 to 1966. Dubinsky was a founder of New York's Liberal Party and was a strong voice for social justice. Under his leadership, the ILGWU spoke out forcefully against the Nazis and in support of the black civil rights movement.

Bottom left: Arthur Goldberg served as attorney for the Congress of Industrial Organizations (CIO) and the United Steel Workers of America. In 1961 he became President Kennedy's Secretary of Labor. He served on the U.S. Supreme Court and as this nation's ambassador to the United Nations.

Bottom right: Actor and television star, Edward Asner, became president of the Screen Actors Guild in 1982.

March 1985: At the Soviet Mission in New York, rabbis blow shofars to protest the treatment of Soviet Jews.

V·RAISED JEWISH VOICES

Cry aloud, without restraint,
Raise your voice like a ram's horn. . . .
To unlock the fetters of wickedness,
And untie the cords of the yoke,
To let the oppressed go free.
Isaiah 58:1,6

קְרָא בְגָרוֹן אַל־תַּחְשֹׂךְ
כַּשּׁוֹפָר הָרֵם קוֹלֶךָ . . . .
פַּתֵּחַ חַרְצֻבּוֹת רֶשַׁע
הַתֵּר אֲגֻדּוֹת מוֹטָה
וְשַׁלַּח רְצוּצִים חָפְשִׁים.

The prophets of ancient Israel denounced injustice. They warned that it is not enough to observe Jewish rituals without also living by the values of the Torah. The God of Israel, the prophets said, is a God of justice and compassion. So, too, must the Jewish people be just and compassionate. Consideration for the poor and sensitivity to human rights are central to prophetic teaching. To be a good Jew, one must have a social conscience.

In the twentieth century, American Jews have lived through a number of events of great moral, political, and social significance. Among these are the Holocaust, the creation of the State of Israel, and the Black civil rights movement. These events have required Jews to "cry aloud, without restraint," to raise their voices "like a ram's horn." (Isaiah 58:1)

Civil disobedience has been a part of the Jewish heritage since the midwives ignored pharaoh's order to kill all Jewish male babies. (Exodus 1:17) Modern Jews, expelled from the Soviet embassy when they protest the mistreatment of their fellow Jews in the Soviet Union, are reliving the experience of the prophet Amos, who was banished from the king's sanctuary because of his revolutionary ideas. (Amos 7:13) Jews who are arrested because they participate in civil rights activities are following in the footsteps of the prophet Jeremiah, who was beaten and put in prison when he spoke out against unjust authorities. (Jeremiah 20:2; 32:2)

The United States Constitution guarantees the right of free speech. Americans may argue, march, demonstrate, protest, strike, and confront their government in an attempt to influence its laws and change its policies. It is a right that Jewish Americans have used frequently. Throughout their history as a people scattered among the nations of the world, Jews have never before felt at home enough to speak their thoughts loudly and without fear. These raised Jewish voices proclaim the uniqueness of the Jewish experience in America.

CHAPTER ONE
AMERICAN JEWRY DURING THE NAZI ERA

The Rise of Nazi Germany

When Adolf Hitler came to power in Germany in 1933, he began to persecute that nation's Jews. There were boycotts of Jewish businesses. Jews were barred from holding government jobs, being doctors, lawyers, or reporters. Jews who were naturalized Germans lost their citizenship. Kosher slaughter of animals was forbidden. Eventually, hundreds of laws were passed that deprived German Jews of their rights.

The boycott of Jewish stores, Berlin, 1933.

Quiet Diplomacy

There were Jews in America who opposed any open protest against these German actions. Some felt that protest was unnecessary because the Nazis would not remain in power. Others were afraid that the Nazis might react to foreign protests by making life even harder for Germany's Jews. Still others thought that demonstrations on behalf of German Jews would be embarrassing and might lead to a rise in anti-Semitism in the United States. These people believed that American Jews should either do nothing or try to influence American policy quietly, through closed meetings with government leaders.

Public Protests

There were also American Jews who did not hesitate to speak out on behalf of their fellow Jews in Germany. Among the first were the Jewish War Veterans, who paraded on March 23, 1933 to protest the persecution of German Jews. A few days later, on March 27th, anti-Nazi rallies were held in eighty cities across the nation, including New

The Jewish War Veterans marching in support of a boycott of German goods.

A mass demonstration and parade protesting German anti-Semitism (New York, 1933).

Rabbi Stephen S. Wise, President of the American Jewish Congress, addressing an anti-Nazi rally in New York. Wise recognized the Nazi menace and organized protests against it. He said: "What is happening in Germany may happen tomorrow in any other land on earth unless it is challenged. . . . We must speak out."

York, Philadelphia, Baltimore, Boston, Cleveland, and Chicago. Such mass demonstrations were held throughout the Nazi era.

Activist Jews also protested Nazi policies with economic pressure, organizing a boycott of German goods. They carried signs that said, "For Humanity's Sake, Don't Buy German Goods." They walked picket lines in front of Macy's, Sears, Woolworth's, and other stores to shame them into honoring the boycott.

Immigration Quotas and Restrictions

American Jews also tried to change America's immigration laws, so that victims of Nazi persecution could escape to this country. The gates of immigration, through which millions had entered the United States, were now closed. In 1924, Congress had enacted laws restricting immigration. The American public favored these laws, especially during the Great Depression of the thirties, when many people feared that new immigrants would deprive them of jobs. The new laws set limits, or quotas, on how many citizens of each foreign nation could come. It became extremely difficult to get a visa to come to America. In spite of pleas by Jewish leaders, attempts to change immigration laws were largely unsuccessful.

A 1933 demonstration in Chicago to protest the Nazis' burning of books by Jews and other "undesirables."

An announcement for a 1937 demonstration against the Nazis, sponsored by the Joint Boycott Council of the American Jewish Congress and the Jewish Labor Committee.

The problem of quotas was complicated by the State Department, which controlled the issuance of visas. Many papers were required and applicants often had to wait years—sometimes in vain—to get permission to come to America. Whether it was because they personally disliked Jews or were supporters of the anti-immigration policy, State Department officials made it hard to get visas. Sometimes quotas were not even filled, although hundreds of thousands of people were seeking admission to this country.

Among those leaving the White House after a 1938 conference on refugees from Nazism are Rabbi Stephen Wise and Jewish financier and diplomat, Henry Morgenthau, Sr. (third and fourth from left). Although Wise was a personal friend of Franklin Roosevelt's, he never persuaded the president to take forceful action to save Europe's Jews.

Under the vigorous leadership of its president, David Dubinsky, the International Ladies Garment Workers Union was outspoken in its campaign against Nazi Germany.

An illustration from a 1938 leaflet put out by the Joint Distribution Committee, which was raising money to help the Jews of Europe fight the Nazi threat.

1,000,000 JEWS SLAIN BY NAZIS, REPORT SAYS

'Slaughterhouse' of Europe Under Hitler Described at London

LONDON, June 29 (U.P.) — The Germans have massacred more than 1,000,000 Jews since the war began in carrying out Adolf Hitler's proclaimed policy of exterminating the people, spokesmen for the World Jewish Congress charged today.

They said the Nazis had established a "vast slaughterhouse for Jews" in Eastern Europe and that reliable reports showed that 700,-000 Jews already had been murdered in Lithuania and Poland, 125,000 in Rumania, 200,000 in Nazi-occupied parts of Russia and 100,000 in the rest of Europe. Thus about one-sixth of the pre-war Jewish population in Europe, estimated at 6,000,000 to 7,000,000 persons, had been wiped out in less than three years.

A report to the congress said that Jews, deported en masse to Central Poland from Germany, Austria, Czechoslovakia and the Netherlands, were being shot by firing squads at the rate of 1,000 daily.

Information received by the Polish Government in London confirmed that the Nazis had executed "several hundred thousand" Jews in Poland and that almost another million were imprisoned in ghettos.

The Years of Mass Murder

By 1942, President Roosevelt and the State Department knew for sure what some members of the public were beginning to suspect but had trouble believing: Hitler was murdering the Jews of Europe. "Stop Hitler Now" rallies were held throughout the nation. Newspaper ads were placed to influence public opinion. Petitions were presented to government leaders. The American Joint Distribution Committee increased its relief and rescue operations in Europe.

American Jews continued to press their government to help European Jewry, but it was not until 1944 that President Roosevelt agreed to set up the War Refugee Board. Its purpose was to develop programs and to take diplomatic action to help victims of the Nazis. Within a year, the board was able to rescue hundreds of thousands of people.

On October 6, 1943, 500 orthodox rabbis marched on Washington, requesting help for the victims of Nazism. After President Roosevelt refused to meet with them, Eliezer Silver and Wolf Gold presented their petition to Vice-President Henry Wallace (left).

On June 30, 1942, The New York Times reported that more than a million Jews had been murdered by the Nazis. This copy of the story has been enlarged many times, for easy reading. The actual article was only a few inches long and was buried in the middle of the newspaper. Many Americans found these stories of German death camps hard to believe. It was not until after the war, when the camps were liberated, that people realized the horrible truth.

The Last March, *by sculptor Nathan Rapoport, is part of the Holocaust Memorial Wall at the Jewish Theological Seminary of America.*

Why Couldn't They Help?

Why were America's Jews unable to persuade their government to rescue the Jews of Europe?

Many people—both Jews and non-Jews—thought the stories of mass murder in Europe were exaggerated. They simply did not believe that anyone was capable of such horrible deeds, so they did not understand the need for action.

The Jewish community of the thirties and early forties was poorly organized. There were conflicts between the Orthodox, Conservative, and Reform movements; between Zionists and anti-Zionists; between the committees that favored big demonstrations and newspaper ads and those that believed in quiet pressure on the government. The Jews did not speak as one, and as a result, their voices were weak. But even if they had been united, would they have been able to influence the government?

The nation was concentrating on winning the war as quickly as possible. Many people in government believed that trying to save Jewish lives would slow the war effort. For this reason, and for others we may never understand, the State Department did everything it could to suppress information about the "final solution" and even sabotaged rescue efforts.

Perhaps the ultimate reason why America's Jews did not succeed in rescuing more of Hitler's victims was that they lacked power. Try as they might to influence their government to help, the final decision was not up to them. It rested with President Roosevelt and with Congress and they refused to act until it was too late.

This photograph shows a scene of mass executions committed by the Nazis.

CLOSE-UPS: *Their Brothers' Keepers*

Cecilia Razovsky

Although the passengers had landing certificates from Cuba's immigration department, they were not allowed off the ship. Officials of the agency pleaded with the Cubans, offering them money and a guarantee that the refugees would not take jobs away from Cubans. It was a tense period. In a letter to the agency's New York office, Razovsky wrote that she had been sending messages to the ship's passengers three times daily, "to keep up their courage and to prevent catastrophes. For as time goes on," she continued, "they are getting very much alarmed." Both Cuba and the United States refused to admit the refugees, who returned to an uncertain fate in Europe.

FIGHTING IMMIGRATION RESTRICTIONS

Cecilia Razovsky was a trained social worker who became an expert on immigration problems while working for the Department of Immigrant Aid of the National Council of Jewish Women. In 1934 she became executive director of German Jewish Children's Aid, a group that tried to arrange for German children to be cared for in American homes.

Razovsky's attempt to get visas for the children was opposed by anti-immigration forces. Although she was able to get permission for two hundred fifty children to enter in 1934, only a hundred children were admitted each year after that. By contrast, over eight thousand German-Jewish children were admitted to Great Britain in 1939 alone.

In May 1939, Razovsky was sent to Cuba by the Joint Distribution Committee, to prepare housing and schooling facilities for over nine hundred German refugees arriving on a ship called the *St. Louis*.

WOMEN ON THE HOME FRONT

Members of the Women's Division of the American Jewish Congress campaigned actively against the Nazis. They organized picket lines in front of stores that violated the boycott of German goods, and they arranged for publication of books and pamphlets to arouse public opinion against the Nazis. These efforts so angered the Germans that the Nazi press referred to the Women's Division as "women of the street," meaning prostitutes. When this happened, Louise Waterman Wise, the division's president, convinced the State Department to file a formal protest with the German Foreign Office.

During the thirties, the Women's Division opened Congress Houses, temporary homes that sheltered thousands of refugees. A volunteer staff worked to make the refugees feel at home. Others collected money and clothing for the refugees and for the needy in Europe. When the war broke out, the Division ran Congress Defense Houses that provided hospitality for servicemen.

In 1946, Razovsky (in uniform) went to Bremen, Germany, to help these refugees deal with American immigration procedures.

Louise Waterman Wise (left) with Women's Division volunteers sewing clothing for refugees from Nazi Germany.

A RELIEF WORKER IMPRISONED IN SHANGHAI

Laura Margolis worked on the overseas staff of the Joint Distribution Committee. In 1939 she worked with German refugees stranded in Cuba. In May 1941, she was sent to the Japanese-held city of Shanghai. Together with Manuel Siegel, she used Joint funds to give food, clothing, shelter, and medical attention to thousands of refugees from Nazi-occupied Europe.

In December 1941, the United States entered the war. The Joint had to stop sending money and communications to Shanghai because it was held by the Japanese and was now enemy territory. Working under difficult conditions, Margolis and Siegel managed to provide a daily meal for over eight thousand refugees. Each day they expected to be arrested as enemy aliens. Early in 1943, their fears were realized and they were sent to a Japanese detention camp.

Although Siegel remained in the camp until after the liberation of Shanghai, Margolis was released in September 1943, as part of a prisoner-of-war exchange. She went to Spain, where she worked in secret operations to rescue European children. Her next assignment was Sweden, where she set up a system for sending packages to people imprisoned in concentration camps. After the war, Margolis became chief of Joint's relief operations in France, where she met and married Marc Jarblum. Eventually they made *aliyah* to Israel, where for many years Margolis continued working for the Joint.

Laura Margolis after her release from the Japanese detention camp in Shanghai (1943).

"SCHWARTZ OF THE JOINT"

The American Joint Distribution Committee ("the Joint") was founded in 1914 to provide relief for the Jews of war-torn Europe. During the Nazi era, most Jewish-American relief and rescue efforts were carried out through the Joint.

Joseph J. Schwartz (left) in Marseilles, France, with a European-Jewish relief worker (1941).

Both during and after World War II, the Joint's European operations were directed by Joseph J. Schwartz. To hundreds of thousands of Europe's Jews, "Schwartz of the Joint" was their guardian angel. Joint funds kept over ten thousand Jewish children alive, and in hiding, in France. The Joint transferred money to Jewish resistance groups, provided false passports and sent food packages. The Joint even entered into indirect negotiations with the Nazis in attempts to pay ransom for the Jews of Europe. Faced with a hopeless task, the Joint's staff managed to save about eighty thousand Jews from the clutches of the Nazis. The Joint also provided much of the financing for the work of the War Refugee Board.

From 1945 to 1952, the Joint spent over $342 million to help the victims of war. Schwartz supervised the relief programs and helped hundreds of thousands of refugees emigrate to the United States, Canada, Latin America, and Palestine. He participated in the rescue of Kurdish Jews from northern Iran in 1950, and in Operation Magic Carpet, the migration of fifty thousand Yemenite Jews to Israel.

Schwartz presiding at the International Conference on Jewish Relief and Rehabilitation, Paris, December 1948.

MORGENTHAU PERSUADES THE PRESIDENT

Henry Morgenthau, Jr. was the United States Secretary of the Treasury from 1934 to 1945. In 1943 Morgenthau learned that the State Department had proof of the mass murder of European Jews and had kept this information secret. Shocked by his discovery, he ordered a thorough investigation.

His assistants prepared a report that condemned some officials of the State Department and accused them of preventing the rescue of Jews. The report charged that these officials had blocked the efforts of private organizations to save Jews and had made it almost impossible for refugees to get visas.

Morgenthau presented this report to President Roosevelt on January 16, 1944. He added that many people saw "plain anti-Semitism motivating the actions of these State Department officials," and warned the president that the situation could "explode into a nasty scandal." Morgenthau suggested the establishment of a War Refugee Board, to take the problem of rescue of Jews from the control of the State Department.

Roosevelt must have realized that if this report were made public, it would damage him politically. Six days after his meeting with Morgenthau, he announced the creation of the board. Its job was to rescue victims of the Nazis and to establish temporary shelters for them. It saved thousands of Jews.

Ira Hirschmann

A RESCUER IN TURKEY

In 1944 Ira Hirschmann went to Turkey where, as a special representative of President Roosevelt and the War Refugee Board, he was able to rescue thousands of Jews in Rumania, Bulgaria, and Hungary.

Soon after his arrival in Turkey, Hirschmann met with the Rumanian ambassador. Hirschmann promised him four American visas for his family in exchange for his help in persuading his government to release Jews from concentration camps in Rumania. The ambassador agreed, and in March 1944, forty-eight thousand camp inmates were released. Hirschmann also

Henry Morgenthau, Jr.

Hirschmann (right) in Istanbul, 1944, with some of the children he helped free from concentration camps. They are on their way to be smuggled into Palestine.

persuaded the Bulgarian government to cancel its anti-Semitic laws affecting the forty-five thousand Jews still left in that country.

Using money donated by the Joint and the U.S. government, Hirschmann hired ships to carry Jews from Constanza in Rumania to Istanbul, Turkey. From there, he arranged for thousands of refugees to travel by train to Palestine.

Together with the Vatican's delegate to Turkey, Monsignor Angelo Roncalli (later Pope John XXIII), Hirschmann arranged for Hungarian Jews to undergo fake baptisms. They were then provided with false papers that ''proved'' they were Christians. The understanding was that once they were out of danger, the ''converts'' would return to Judaism. In this way, thousands of Hungarian Jews were saved from the Nazis.

MOTHER RUTH AND HER ONE THOUSAND REFUGEES

In May 1944, Treasury Secretary Morgenthau suggested to President Roosevelt that refugees be offered shelter in the United States. The President agreed to make a small gesture. On June 12, he signed a special order allowing one thousand refugees to enter this country on a temporary basis. They were to be kept in an old army camp in Oswego, New York, and were to be returned to Europe when the war ended.

Ruth Gruber worked at the Department of the Interior, which was to run the camp. She volunteered to bring the refugees to America. She spoke German and Yiddish and knew that she could help the refugees. Because she was young and a woman, many objected to sending her. But Harold Ickes, the Secretary of the Interior, decided to let her go. She went to Italy as his representative and escorted the refugees to the United States.

Ruth Gruber (right) with two Red Cross workers on the ship that brought the refugees to America.

During the voyage by ship to America, Gruber took notes on the refugees' experiences. She heard about the concentration camps, about torture and starvation, and about people being murdered. Gruber knew that these were the first wartime witnesses to come to America and it was important that the world learn their stories.

Gruber, who became known as ''Mother Ruth,'' went with the refugees to the camp and helped them settle in. The refugees remained in Oswego until after the war. Most of them were allowed to stay in America.

Members of B'nai B'rith presenting a Torah to the refugees, so that services could be held on the first Friday night at the camp. Gruber watches as the Torah is held by one of the refugees, Rabbi Mossco Tzechoval.

FROM OUR JEWISH HERITAGE:
The Responsibility of One Jew for Another

*When their lives are in danger, as they were during
the Holocaust, Jews have always turned to other Jews
for help. What does our heritage teach us about
the responsibility Jews have for each other?*

We Are One

"The Lord our God, the Lord is One," say
the words of the *Sh'ma*. Just as God is One,
so are the children of Israel one. Each individual Jew is a part of the whole, a member of the community of Israel.

Throughout their history, Jews have faced
persecution and oppression and they have
learned that there is great strength in unity.
The Talmud says, "Single reeds can be broken, but many reeds bound together in one
bundle, who can break them?" This solidarity has helped the children of Israel to sur-
vive in an unfriendly world.

Ransoming of Captives

One of the ways in which the Jewish people
have shown their solidarity is by rescuing
fellow Jews who have been captured by
robbers, slave dealers, or political enemies.
This is called *pidyon shevuyim*, ransoming
of captives.

Ransoming captives is of such importance that when Rabbi Phineas ben Yair
went to perform this deed, the river parted
so that he could cross it. The duty to ransom captives even has priority over giving
charity to the poor, according to Maimonides. Money that is supposed to be used for

*This detail from the Arch of Titus
in Rome shows the spoils of Jerusalem being carried off by the
Romans in 70 C.E. Judea was
conquered, the Temple in Jerusalem was destroyed, and thousands
of Jews were sent into slavery.
Pidyon shevuyim would have required that, if possible, the captives be rescued. The value that we
place on the lives of our people
was shown in May 1985, when the
Israeli government released more
than a thousand terrorists in exchange for three Israeli prisoners-
of-war who were being held by the
Arabs.*

a charitable or religious purpose, such as the building of a synagogue, may be used to ransom captives. If someone does not ransom another Jew as quickly as possible, it is as though he had spilled the blood of the captive Jew.

Pidyon Shevuyim Today

In every generation, there are Jewish communities in crisis. While they may not be held for a ransom involving money, they are still in captivity. They may be persecuted because they are Jews. They may be forbidden to practice their religion. They may not be allowed to go to the land of Israel.

If one Jew suffers, all Jews should feel the pain. All Jews are responsible for one another. If a fellow Jew is in need of rescue, the religious duty of pidyon shevuyim requires that all Jews take action.

A poster for the annual "Solidarity Sunday," when hundreds of thousands of Jewish-Americans across the nation march to show support for Soviet Jews.

In 1969, eleven Iraqi Jews were accused of spying and executed. American Jews joined worldwide demonstrations against the Iraqi government.

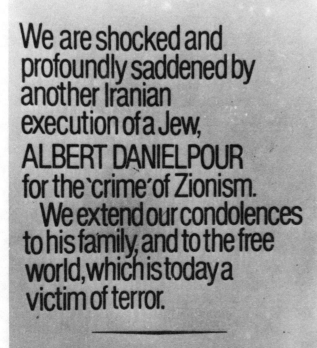

We are shocked and profoundly saddened by another Iranian execution of a Jew, ALBERT DANIELPOUR for the 'crime' of Zionism.
    We extend our condolences to his family, and to the free world, which is today a victim of terror.

Anti-Defamation League of B'nai B'rith
823 United Nations Plaza, New York, NY 10017

After an Iranian Jew was executed by the government of Ayatollah Khomeini, this statement of protest was issued by the Anti-Defamation League of B'nai B'rith.

America's Jews often participate in demonstrations to influence American public opinion in favor of Israel. Here, they are protesting against the terrorist tactics of the Palestine Liberation Organization.

The Nazi Era   175

JEWISH COMMUNITIES IN CRISIS

Stephen Shalom, a leader of the Syrian-Jewish community in Brooklyn, and Stephen J. Solarz, who represents the district in Congress, conferring with President Jimmy Carter about the problems facing the oppressed Jewish community in Syria.

Below: An advertisement to raise funds for Jews in Ethiopia. The government of Ethiopia would not allow Jews to teach their children about Judaism, to worship freely, or to go to Israel. In the mid-1980s, famine throughout Ethiopia increased the community's tragic plight.

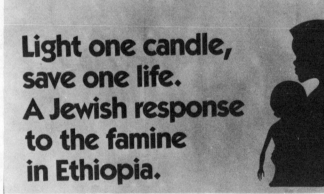

Light one candle, save one life. A Jewish response to the famine in Ethiopia.

Evgeny, Vili, Evgenia, and Dimitri Palanker are "refuseniks," Soviet citizens who have been denied permission to emigrate to Israel. They are standing in their home, in front of a sign reading "Let my people go that they may serve Me." (Exodus 9:1) This photo was taken by an American tourist, one of many who visited refuseniks in an attempt to form a lifeline between them and the Jews of the West.

CHAPTER TWO
AMERICAN JEWS AND THE CREATION OF THE STATE OF ISRAEL

The Zionist Movement

In 1897, Zionists from all over the world came to Basel, Switzerland, for the First Zionist Congress. Jews had always hoped and prayed for a return to the Holy Land. Now they began to work for it as well. Under the leadership of Theodor Herzl, the founder of

the Zionist movement, the World Zionist Organization was established. The main purpose of this political action group was to urge world leaders to support the Zionist goal: "a publicly recognized, legally secured home in Palestine" for the Jewish people.

In 1891, Adam Rosenberg organized the Shavei Zion Society in New York, a group of American Jews who wanted to emigrate to the Holy Land. He made several trips to Palestine to buy land and create settlements for American immigrants. Rosenberg attended the First Zionist Congress. He addressed the delegates on the state of American Jewry and the situation in Palestine.

Rosa Fassel Sonneschein was at the First Zionist Congress as an observer and journalist. Sonneschein was founder and editor of The American Jewess, the first independent magazine in English for Jewish-American women. She was among the first in this country to publish the writings of Theodor Herzl.

Rabbi Shepsel Schaffer was president of the Zion Association of Baltimore, an organization that sent money and supplies to colonies in Palestine. Schaffer was the only official delegate from the U.S. to the First Zionist Congress.

American Opposition to Zionism

Most American Jews were not that enthusiastic about Zionism. Some were afraid that the movement for a Jewish state would make Christians question the loyalty of America's Jews. How could they be good Americans and still support a Jewish nation six thousand miles away?

Ultra-orthodox Jews believed there would be a return to the Holy Land only when the Messiah came. They rejected human efforts to establish a Jewish state.

In the Reform movement, there was also strong opposition to Zionism. Its Pittsburgh Platform of 1885 stated that Jews were "no longer a nation, but a religious community," and that they should not expect "a return to Palestine." In spite of its anti-Zionist views, the Reform movement produced such noted American Zionists as Stephen S. Wise and Abba Hillel Silver. Eventually, the official Reform stand on Zionism changed. According to the "Guiding Principles of Reform Judaism" issued in 1937, all Jews must help rebuild Palestine "as a Jewish homeland" and make it "a haven of refuge for the oppressed [and] a center of Jewish culture and spiritual life."

The Growth of American Zionism

It was Hitler's persecution of the Jews of Europe that made people sympathetic to the Zionist cause. They realized that if a free Jewish state existed in Palestine, many of Hitler's victims could be saved. But Great Britain controlled Palestine and had decided to restrict Jewish immigration there, even during the war. American Zionists urged U.S. leaders to pressure the British into opening the doors of Palestine, so that Jewish refugees from Nazi Europe would have a place to go. But they were not successful

Louis D. Brandeis, a Boston lawyer, (center) was convinced that Jews would assimilate and disappear unless there was a Jewish homeland. In 1914, Brandeis became chairman of the Provisional Committee for General Zionist Affairs. "Let no American imagine that Zionism is inconsistent with patriotism," he said. "To be good Americans, we must be better Jews, and to be better Jews, we must become Zionists." To his right is Stephen S. Wise and to his left, the philanthropist Nathan Straus.

at this task, partly because the State Department claimed that it would embarrass our British allies and hurt the war effort.

Zionists therefore concentrated their efforts on persuading the American public—both Jewish and non-Jewish—to support the idea of a Jewish state, to be established after the war was over. Zionists set up a network of committees across the nation to educate the public and to present a continuous, united voice on Zionist issues in Washington. Meetings were held with members of Congress to brief them on the Palestine issue. Delegations were sent to Presidents Roosevelt and Truman, to urge their support of Zionist goals. Letter-writing campaigns were mounted, and Zionist speakers were sent out to win over the public.

The success of the effort to "Zionize" America's Jews may be seen in the membership rolls of the leading Zionist organizations. Between 1940 and 1948, the Zionist Organization of America grew from 49,000 members to 225,000. Membership in Hadassah, the Women's Zionist Organization of America, tripled during this period. And among the non-Jewish public, in 1944 alone, more than 3,000 organizations, including church groups and labor unions, passed pro-Zionist resolutions and sent telegrams of support to Congress.

During a 1944 campaign to sell American war bonds, the Zionist Organization of America pledged to sell $25 million in bonds. Zionist loyalty to America was so strong that the ZOA succeeded in raising more than $68 million for the war effort.

A delegation of Jewish leaders meeting with President Truman.

The Partition Plan

After the war, there were thousands of Jewish survivors in the camps of Europe. The need for a Jewish homeland was greater than ever. A plan was proposed in the United Nations that Palestine be divided into two nations, one Arab and one Jewish. The Zionists supported this partition plan because they realized it was the only way the world would agree to the establishment of a Jewish state.

In America, a massive campaign was mounted to persuade President Truman and Congress to support the partition plan. Truman later said, "I do not think I ever had as much pressure and propaganda aimed at the White House as I had in this instance." The President was aware that he would need the Jewish vote in his 1948 re-election cam-

President Truman with his friend and former business partner, Eddie Jacobson (left). Jacobson was able to persuade Truman to see Zionist leaders such as Chaim Weizmann and Arthur Lelyveld (Chairman of the Committee on Unity for Palestine), who urged the president to support the Zionist position.

Rose Halprin, a member of the Jewish Agency delegation to the United Nations, talking to Cuban U.N. ambassador Guillermo Belt, in May 1947.

In 1945, the U.S. government sent Earl Harrison to inspect the camps housing Holocaust survivors. Army chaplain Abraham J. Klausner (third from left, with Dachau inmates) went with him and made sure that Harrison saw the horrible conditions in the camps. Harrison wrote that America was treating the Jews as badly "as the Nazis treated them except that we do not exterminate them." Truman underlined this sentence in Harrison's report, which helped convince him that the Jewish refugees needed a homeland in Palestine.

Israel Goldstein, former president of the Zionist Organization of America (1943–45) hugging Jewish Agency delegate to the U.N., Abba Hillel Silver, after the successful U.N. vote on partition.

paign. But he was also a humane man and he was deeply affected by the plight of the Jewish refugees. Over the objections of the pro-Arab State Department, Truman ordered the American delegation to the United Nations to vote for the partition plan.

A Jewish Homeland

On November 29, 1947, the partition plan was brought before the United Nations for a vote. As the first nation was called upon to voice its view, a cry of prayer was heard from the spectators' gallery: "*Ana Adonai hoshiya!*" "Oh Lord, save us!" The final vote was thirty-three in favor of partition, thirteen (mostly Arab) nations against, and ten abstentions.

The British were scheduled to leave Palestine by midnight, May 14, 1948. On that day, the State of Israel was proclaimed. Minutes after the proclamation was read in Tel Aviv, Truman announced that the United States had recognized the new Jewish state. The promise of the song *Hatikvah*— "to be a free people in our own land, the land of Zion and Jerusalem"—had come true.

Zionist Activities

Some historians say that political pressure by Zionists was largely responsible for the American government's support of a Jewish state. But political pressure was not all that American Zionists did to show their commitment to the Zionist dream. They donated millions of dollars to aid and defend the Jews of Palestine. They sent food, clothing, and medical supplies. They risked

Goods being shipped to Palestine.

arrest by secretly shipping military equipment to Palestine when Congress prohibited the export of arms to the area. Americans raised money for the ships that brought "illegal" immigrants to Palestine and American crews helped man the ships. Hundreds of Americans went to Israel to fight in the War of Independence.

Jewish-Americans and Israel

For some Jewish-Americans, the establishment of the State of Israel meant an end to the years of exile. They emigrated to the Jewish land and made it their home.

The majority of Jewish-Americans have chosen to remain in the United States. For them, the existence of Israel has required that they balance their loyalty to America with their emotional and spiritual ties to the Holy Land. They have learned how to express these traditional bonds in new ways, such as through association with political action groups on behalf of Israel or financial support of the Jewish state. At the same time, they have kept faith with the American nation that offered shelter to their ancestors and became their home.

Among the hundreds of Americans who fought in the Israeli War of Independence was a West Point graduate, Colonel David "Mickey" Marcus (right). He was made commander of the Jerusalem front, charged with breaking the siege of the city. On the night of June 10, 1948, Marcus was killed accidentally by one of his own guards.

Fund-raising: Rose Halprin speaking at opening ceremonies of the Hadassah Medical School (1949).

Political Support: Over 100,000 people gathered at the United Nations in November, 1974. They were protesting the invitation to Yasser Arafat, head of the terrorist Palestine Liberation Organization, to speak before the General Assembly.

Tourism: Thousands of Jewish-Americans travel to Israel each year, renewing their ties with the Holy Land and contributing needed dollars to the Israeli economy.

Living in Israel: Some Americans go to Israel for extended periods, to work or to study. The young woman in the back row taught English to Israeli children.

Organizational Work: Many Americans belong to Zionist organizations, which coordinate activities in support of Israel.

CLOSE-UPS: For the Sake of Zion

Stephen Wise in 1899, with leaders of the Federation of American Zionists, the forerunner of the Zionist Organization of America. Top row, left to right: Louis H. Levin, Zvi Masliansky, I.D. Morrison, Louis Magid. Bottom row: Shepsel Schaffer, Wise, Richard Gottheil, Henry Pereira Mendes.

STEPHEN SAMUEL WISE

In the late 1890s, Rabbi Stephen S. Wise helped found the New York Federation of Zionist Societies and the Federation of American Zionists. In 1898, he was a delegate to the Second Zionist Congress, where he met Theodor Herzl, the father of modern Zionism. Wise agreed to become Secretary of the American Section of the world Zionist movement. This was the beginning of his lifetime of service to the Zionist cause.

Wise served as vice-president of the Zionist Organization of America from 1918–20 and president from 1936–38. He was a founder and president of the American and World Jewish Congresses. One of the most prominent Jewish leaders of his time, he con-

ferred with President Roosevelt on issues of importance to the Jewish people.

Although he often disagreed with other Zionists, Wise always tried to keep the movement unified. In his opening remarks to a Zionist conference in 1942, he said that one of the purposes of the meeting was to unify the Zionist movement so that "we may be enabled to win over an even larger number of American Jews, indeed all American Jews, to the support of the Zionist cause."

In 1907, Wise founded the Free Synagogue in New York. As its rabbi, he was able to preach openly about social issues of the day. He was a founder of the National Association for the Advancement of Colored People (1909), the American Civil Liberties Union (1920), and the Jewish Institute of Religion (1922).

Henrietta Szold as a young woman.

HADASSAH

In 1909, Henrietta Szold visited Palestine and was shocked by the disease and the miserable living conditions she saw there. A few years later, she founded Hadassah, the Women's Zionist Organization of America. The organization's purpose was to increase support for Zionism and to raise money for projects in Palestine.

One of Hadassah's major roles has been to provide medical services in the Holy Land. In 1918, the American Zionist Medical Unit—a group of doctors, nurses, and other health workers organized by Hadassah—went to Palestine. From that small

Stephen Wise

Szold with Youth Aliyah children during the 1930s.

beginning grew Hadassah's medical center in Jerusalem, which now includes a world-famous hospital and medical, nursing, and dental schools.

Another program supported by Hadassah is Youth Aliyah. In 1933, Szold became the first director of Youth Aliyah, a program which rescued German-Jewish children from the Nazis by sending them to Palestine. During the next fifty years, Youth Aliyah helped educate and give job training to more than two hundred thousand children from eighty countries and from disadvantaged homes within Israel.

Today, Hadassah is one of the largest women's volunteer organizations in the United States and one of the largest Zionist organizations in the world. Its members raise millions of dollars each year to support its medical, research, and educational programs.

Rudolf G. Sonneborn

THE SONNEBORN INSTITUTE

On July 1, 1945, a meeting was held at the New York apartment of a wealthy businessman named Rudolf G. Sonneborn. Nineteen men had been invited to form what Sonneborn called "the American arm" of the *Haganah,* the secret Jewish defense force in Palestine.

The group became known as the Sonneborn Institute. It aimed to raise money and obtain supplies for the Haganah. A network of supporters was set up

across the country. By the end of the year, the Institute was raising over $100,000 a week. Its members bought surplus tents, radio sets, and other material from the U.S. Army and Navy. They got boats, planes, jeeps, and arms for the defense of Palestine's Jews.

These supplies were gathered in warehouses in port cities such as New York and Baltimore. They had to be shipped secretly from America to Palestine because of the American embargo. Machinery to make guns was packed in boxes marked "farm machinery." Bullets were put in oil drums with false bottoms and the rest of the drums filled with oil. The Sonneborn Institute also sent many everyday things such as sandbags, barbed wire, cots, raincoats, socks, blankets, flashlights, coats, boots, etc. Its members helped equip the fighting force that would someday become the army of the State of Israel.

David K. Niles with President Truman.

THE PRESIDENTIAL ADMINISTRATIVE ASSISTANT

David K. Niles was a member of the White House staff during the administrations of Presidents Roosevelt and Truman. He became convinced by the Holocaust that a Jewish homeland was necessary, and he tried to influence Truman in favor of the Zionist position. He arranged for Zionist leaders to see Cabinet members and the President. He wrote policy papers relating to European refugees and urged Truman to pressure the British into allowing more Jewish immigrants to enter Palestine.

Behind the scenes, Niles helped organize the American government's campaign to get votes for the passage of the U.N. partition plan and the strategy that led to Israel's admission to the United Nations He also helped guide through Congress the first $100 million loan to the Jewish state.

Truman once said that whenever he talked to Niles about Palestine, Niles would burst into tears because he was so emotionally involved with the subject. When Truman announced American recognition of the new Jewish state, he said to Niles, "You're the first person I called, because I know how much this would mean to you." Niles resigned from Truman's staff in 1951, partly because he wanted to visit Israel as a private citizen.

ABBA HILLEL SILVER

Abba Hillel Silver was born in Lithuania in 1893. As a child, he read many books about Zionism and learned to speak Hebrew fluently. In 1902, the Silver family came to America. While living on the Lower East Side, Silver and his brother Maxwell founded the Dr. Herzl Zion Club, the first Hebrew-speaking Zionist organization for young people in America. Political debates and amateur plays on biblical themes were among its activities.

Silver graduated from Hebrew Union College in 1915. Two years later, he became rabbi at Congregation Tifereth Israel in Cleveland, where he served until his death in 1963.

In 1943, Silver became leader of the American Zionist Emergency Council, which aimed to persuade the American public to support a Jewish national home in Palestine. Silver set up a group of activists to write articles, organize fund-raisers, make speeches, and meet with congressional leaders.

As chairman of the American Section of the Jewish Agency, Silver presented Zionist views on the need for a Jewish homeland to the United Nations. On May 14, 1948, Silver had the honor of informing the General Assembly that a new Jewish state had been established in Israel. He told the delegates that the State of Israel would try to realize "those prophetic ideas of justice, brotherhood, peace and democracy which were first proclaimed by the people of Israel in that very land."

AN AMERICAN ZIONIST DIES FOR ISRAEL

Mendel Math was born in Brooklyn to a family of orthodox Jews who were active Zionists. He was drafted into the U.S. Army in 1944. His unit was posted to the Nazi death camps at Dachau and Buchenwald. When Mendel was ordered to help bury the ashes and bodies of Hitler's victims, he refused. He was a *kohain*, a descendant of the priests of ancient Israel, and Jewish law restricts the contact a kohain may have with the dead. Mendel was brought before a military court. Fortunately, his religious views were respected and the charges against him were dropped.

After the war, Mendel became active in Hapoel Hamizrachi, a religious Zionist organization. He set up a group to help the Haganah and participated in military training exercises for Americans who wanted to serve in Palestine. In March 1948, Mendel himself left for Palestine and joined the Haganah.

Mendel fought at Latrun, one of the few battles lost by Jewish forces. As his unit was retreating, his commander asked soldiers to go back and collect weapons from their dead comrades, because the *Haganah* was very short of arms. Mendel and Jerome Kaplan of Bayonne, New Jersey, volunteered. They returned to the field and were hit by an exploding shell. Their bodies were never found. It was May 13, 1948, the day before Israel's independence was declared. Mendel was twenty-one years old.

Below left: Abba Hillel Silver addressing the United Nations. With him are (left to right) Emanuel Neumann, Moshe Sharett, and Wolf Gold.

Mendel Math

FROM OUR JEWISH HERITAGE: Zionism

*The modern Zionist movement is based on a yearning for
a land in which the Jews lived thousands of years ago.
What does our heritage teach us about the relationship of
Jews to the land of Israel?*

The Years of Exile

When Abraham came to the land of Canaan, the Lord said to him, "To your seed I will give this land." (Genesis 12:7) During the thousands of years that Abraham's descendants, the Jews, have lived outside of their promised land, they never stopped hoping that they would return. On Tishah b'Av (the ninth day of the Hebrew month of Av), observant Jews mourn the destruction of the Temple in Jerusalem, the loss of the Holy Land, and the years of exile. They read aloud from the book of Lamentations that "our inheritance," the land promised to Abraham's seed, "has been passed to

strangers," (5:2) and that the people of Judah have "gone into exile . . . [and] dwell among the nations." (1:3)

In their daily prayers, Jews have turned towards Jerusalem and expressed their hope for a rebirth of their homeland. "If I forget thee, O Jerusalem," said the author of the psalm, "let my right hand forget her cunning." (Psalm 137:5) Both the Yom Kippur service and Pesaḥ seder end with the hope, "Next year in Jerusalem,"—"*L'shanah haba'ah b'Yerushalayim*." The grace after meals includes a plea to God to "rebuild Jerusalem, the Holy City, soon in our days."

A drawing by Saul Raskin, illustrating the yearning for Zion.

Jerusalem reunited and rebuilt (1980).

The Promise of Return

The Bible warned that the children of Israel would be "cast . . . into another land." (Deuteronomy 29:27) It also predicted that the Lord would gather them "from all the peoples" and bring them "to the land which [their] fathers possessed." (Deuteronomy 30:3–5) The prophets repeated the promise that the Jews would be returned to their own land. "And He will assemble the dispersed of Israel . . . from the four corners of the earth," said Isaiah. (11:12) "And I will . . . gather you out of the countries wherein you are scattered . . . I shall bring you into the land of Israel," said the Lord. (Ezekiel 20:34, 42) Throughout the centuries of their separation from their land, the Jews kept their belief in this *kibbutz galuyot*, the gathering of the exiles. This faith in the eventual rebuilding of the nation of Israel was the inspiration of modern Zionism.

Zion of the Spirit

Now that the State of Israel exists and the city of Jerusalem is in Jewish hands, why do Jews continue to pray, "Next year in Jerusalem?" Why is God still asked to "rebuild Jerusalem?" The answer is that when Jews pray for a return to Zion, they mean more than their physical presence in the Holy Land. When they ask God to rebuild Jerusalem, they are not talking about an urban renewal program!

To Jews, Israel is more than a piece of land, Jerusalem is more than a city. Israel and Jerusalem have a spiritual meaning as well. They refer to a world where there is peace and justice, where "the wolf shall dwell with the lamb and the leopard shall lie down with the kid." (Isaiah 11:6) Although the State of Israel has been reborn, Jews continue to hope for the world's spiritual rebirth. "Next year in Jerusalem" is a prayer for a world where "nation shall not lift up sword against nation, neither shall they learn war any more." (Isaiah 2:4; Micah 4:3)

Harry Friedenwald

Although raised and educated in Milwaukee, Golda Meir believed that "a true, free Jewish life" was possible only in the Holy Land. She emigrated to Palestine in 1921 and became a leader in the labor movement and the government. Meir returned to America in 1948 to raise millions of dollars for the defense of Israel. She served as Israeli foreign minister from 1956 to 1965 and as prime minister from 1969 to 1974.

Golda Meir

Harry Friedenwald, a Baltimore eye doctor, was president of the Federation of American Zionists from 1904 to 1918. In 1919, he spent a year in Palestine as chairman of the Zionist Commission, which was the link between the British government and the Jewish population of Palestine, and the predecessor of the Jewish Agency.

Rose Luria Halprin

Julian Mack was chairman of the Jewish delegation to the Versailles peace conference in 1919, where he presented the Zionist position, noting: "We ask no more for the Jews than we do for anyone else." Mack served as president of the Zionist Organization of America and was a founder of the Pro-Palestine Federation of America, an organization whose prupose was to convince Christian clergymen to support Zionism.

Julian Mack

As a member of the Executive of the Jewish Agency-American Section, Rose Luria Halprin participated in the negotiations at the United Nations that led to the creation of the State of Israel. She was chairman of the American Section from 1960 to 1968. Halprin also served as national president of Hadassah from 1932 to 1934 and 1947 to 1952. During her presidency, the decision was made to build a new Hadassah hospital in western Jerusalem. The original facility, on Mount Scopus, fell into Jordanian hands during the War of Independence.

Louis Lipsky, writer and Zionist leader, was one of the founders of the Jewish Agency, the American and World Jewish Congresses. In 1901, he founded *The Maccabean* (later called *The New Palestine*), the main publication of the American Zionist movement. Lipsky was president of the ZOA from 1922 to 1930.

Judith Epstein

Louis Lipsky

Judith Epstein was national president of Hadassah from 1937 to 1939 and 1943 to 1947. She testified before the Anglo-American Commission on Palestine and congressional committees in an effort to persuade government leaders to support a Jewish state. She once said: "Is it too much to ask our own government, friend and champion of the underprivileged and oppressed, to stand forth and demand justice for the Jew through the establishment of a Jewish commonwealth?"

In the 1940s, Emanuel Neumann represented the Jewish Agency in Washington, D.C. He met with leaders of the American and Soviet governments, urging them to support the establishment of a Jewish state. Neumann was a member of the Jewish Agency's delegation to the U.N. during the crucial partition negotiations and was president of the ZOA from 1947 to 1949 and 1956 to 1958.

Tamar de Sola Pool

Emanuel Neumann

As president of Hadassah from 1939 to 1943, Tamar de Sola Pool represented the organization at the Biltmore Conference in 1942, where American Zionists publicly stated their goal of a Jewish state in Palestine. A leader of the World Zionist Organization and Youth Aliyah, Pool went to Cyprus, where she brought in Hadassah teams to educate refugee children in British detention camps.

CHAPTER THREE
JEWS AND THE CIVIL RIGHTS MOVEMENT

"The Call"

On February 12, 1909, the one hundredth anniversary of the birth of Abraham Lincoln, a group of Americans issued a "Call" for a conference on black civil rights. Lincoln had freed the slaves, but blacks still did not have equal opportunities in America. They needed a national organization to protect their rights, and the National Association for the Advancement of Colored People (the "NAACP") was founded. This was the beginning of the modern civil rights movement.

From the start, Jewish-Americans were active in this struggle. Signers of the "Call" included Rabbi Emil Hirsch of Chicago, Rabbi Stephen Wise, and the social workers Lillian Wald and Henry Moskowitz of New York. Brothers Joel and Arthur Spingarn, Martha Gruening, and Herbert Seligmann worked with the NAACP. Among those who donated large sums of money to black causes were Jacob Schiff, Felix Warburg, and the Rosenwald family.

One of the four Jews who signed the "Call" was Henry Moskowitz, a social worker among the immigrants on New York's Lower East Side. Moskowitz and Stephen Wise worked together for over a year to organize a 1910 conference on black voting rights in the South. In 1912, Moskowitz was among those who tried to get the Progressive Party to adopt a civil rights platform.

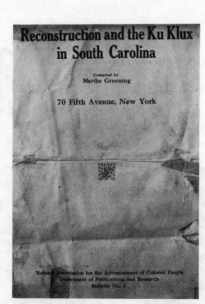

Martha Gruening joined the NAACP staff in 1912. She worked on the anti-lynching campaign and helped publicize the organization's efforts by writing articles and pamphlets such as this one on the Ku Klux Klan.

Joel Elias Spingarn was chairman of the board of the NAACP from 1914 to 1918 and, at the time of his death in 1939, was its president. Black nationalist leader W.E.B. Du Bois described him as one of the "idealists . . . the Jewish race has given the world." Spingarn devoted his life to the civil rights struggle.

Jewish Involvement

Why have so many Jews been active in the civil rights movement? Some say this was a natural outgrowth of the Jewish tradition of social justice. The Torah commands, "Justice, justice, shall ye pursue." (Deuteronomy 16:20) The word "justice" is repeated, according to the rabbis, to teach that one must seek justice not only for Jews, but for non-Jews as well.

Black leader Roy Wilkins thought that Jews were involved in the movement because "Jewish people understand this business of discrimination. . . . They have great sympathy for those who are fighting it." Wilkins was suggesting that because Jews had suffered and been persecuted themselves, they were ready to help another oppressed minority group. Jews also realized that discrimination against blacks often meant discrimination against Jews as well. They hoped that their efforts on behalf of blacks would also benefit the Jews.

Jewish Lawyers and Civil Rights

Some of the most important battles in the struggle for black equality took place in the courtroom. Lawsuits were fought on behalf of blacks who were not given fair trials, who were prevented from serving on juries, from voting, from buying houses in white neighborhoods, or attending white schools. Among the first of the many Jewish lawyers who offered their services to the civil rights movement was Arthur Spingarn. In 1913 he took charge of the NAACP's legal department and was its unpaid director for more than twenty-five years. Other Jews who worked as lawyers or legal advisers on civil rights cases included Louis Marshall, Louis Brandeis, Felix Frankfurter, Arthur Garfield Hays, Morris Ernst, and Jack Greenberg.

There were hotels, clubs, housing developments, and schools that discriminated against both blacks and Jews. This 1905 ad for a Massachusetts hotel reads, "We have no HEBREW patronage." It was understood that no blacks would be allowed either.

Arthur B. Spingarn was president of the NAACP from 1940 to 1966 and director of its legal department for more than 25 years.

The well-known constitutional lawyer Louis Marshall worked with the NAACP's legal committee on cases involving the right of blacks to vote and to buy homes in white neighborhoods.

The new, modern school for whites and the old, broken-down school for blacks in South Park, Kansas.

The "lunchroom" at the black school in South Park.

Nathan Margold

Equal Education for Blacks

In 1929, a lawyer named Nathan Margold was hired by the NAACP to make a study of the legal status of blacks. Margold understood that equality for blacks depended largely on quality education for black children. He devoted much of his report to a discussion of discrimination in public schools.

In an 1896 case, the U.S. Supreme Court had held that "separate but equal" facilities for blacks were legal. The Margold Report urged the NAACP to "boldly challenge the constitutional validity of segregation" where the separate schools for blacks did not actually provide equal educational opportunities. For example, whites often attended beautiful, modern schools, while blacks studied in old, crumbling buildings.

The courtroom attack on segregated schools was led by Thurgood Marshall, the noted black lawyer who directed the NAACP Legal Defense Fund. To Marshall's team of lawyers, the Margold Report was "the Bible of the NAACP legal drive."

Standing on the steps of the Supreme Court are four of the lawyers who argued Brown and related cases: (left to right) Jack Greenberg, Thurgood Marshall, Louis Redding, and U. Simpson Tate. Greenberg joined the staff of the NAACP Legal Defense Fund in 1949 and became its director when Marshall left. Greenberg won more than forty Supreme Court cases involving issues such as equal education and employment discrimination.

IN THE
Supreme Court of the United States
October Term, 1952

No. 8

OLIVER BROWN, MRS. RICHARD LAWTON,
MRS. SADIE EMMANUEL, ET AL.,
Appellants,

VS.

BOARD OF EDUCATION OF TOPEKA, SHAWNEE
COUNTY, KANSAS, ET AL.

**On Appeal from the United States District Court
for the District of Kansas**

**BRIEF OF AMERICAN JEWISH CONGRESS
AS AMICUS CURIAE**

HERMAN L. WEISMAN,
SHAD POLIER,
WILL MASLOW,
JOSEPH B. ROBISON,
Attorneys for
AMERICAN JEWISH CONGRESS,
15 East 84th Street,
New York 28, N. Y.

Among the organizations that filed papers supporting the black position in the Brown case was the American Jewish Congress, which wrote: "Through the thousands of years of our tragic history we have learned . . . [that] the persecution . . . of any minority [means] persecution of all minorities. . . . Our immediate objective here is to secure unconditional equality for Americans of Negro ancestry. Our ultimate objective in this case, as in all others, is to preserve the dignity of all men so that we may achieve full equality in a free society."

The Supreme Court Speaks

A major victory in the struggle against discrimination in education came in 1954, when the Supreme Court decided the case of *Brown* versus *Board of Education*. The Court ruled that segregation of children in public schools was illegal.

Among the Jewish organizations to voice their immediate support of the decision was Women's League for Conservative Judaism, which asked its Sisterhoods to "do all that lies within their power" to see that the decision was carried out.

In the Sixties

When Martin Luther King, Jr. told the world, "I have a dream," many Jews tried to help make that dream come true. Between 1963 and 1966, hundreds of Jews went down South to help register black voters, open community centers for blacks, and teach black children in "freedom schools." Some of these volunteers were motivated by the lack of action on behalf of Jews during the Holocaust. As a student from the Bronx who worked in Mississippi said, "This is the kind of fight that should have been fought thirty years ago." Others wanted to participate in what one rabbi who went to Birmingham called "the last phase of the American Civil War."

Individually and through their community organizations, Jewish-Americans picketed against segregation, filed court papers supporting black legal battles, marched against poverty, and raised money to support the civil rights movement. In a 1966 survey, when blacks were asked what group outside of the black community had done the most for blacks, Jews were at the top of the list.

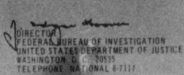

MISSING **CALL FBI**

THE FBI IS SEEKING INFORMATION CONCERNING THE DISAPPEARANCE AT PHILADELPHIA, MISSISSIPPI OF THESE THREE INDIVIDUALS ON JUNE 21 1964 EXTENSIVE INVESTIGATION IS BEING CONDUCTED TO LOCATE GOODMAN, CHANEY, AND SCHWERNER, WHO ARE DESCRIBED AS FOLLOWS:

	ANDREW GOODMAN	JAMES EARL CHANEY	MICHAEL HENRY SCHWERNER
RACE:	White	Negro	White
SEX:	Male	Male	Male
DOB:	November 23, 1943	May 30, 1943	November 6, 1939
POB:	New York City	Meridian, Mississippi	New York City
AGE:	20 years	21 years	24 years
HEIGHT:	5'10"	5'7"	5'9" to 5'10"
WEIGHT:	150 pounds	135 to 140 pounds	170 to 180 pounds
HAIR:	Dark brown, wavy	Black	Brown
EYES:	Brown	Brown	Light blue
TEETH:	Good; none missing		
SCARS AND MARKS:	1 inch cut scar 2 inches above left ear		Pock mark center of forehead, slight scar on bridge of nose, appendectomy scar, broken leg scar.

SHOULD YOU HAVE OR IN THE FUTURE RECEIVE ANY INFORMATION CONCERNING THE WHEREABOUTS OF THESE INDIVIDUALS, YOU ARE REQUESTED TO NOTIFY ME OR THE NEAREST OFFICE OF THE FBI. TELEPHONE NUMBER IS LISTED BELOW.

DIRECTOR
FEDERAL BUREAU OF INVESTIGATION
UNITED STATES DEPARTMENT OF JUSTICE
WASHINGTON, D.C. 20535
TELEPHONE NATIONAL 8-7117

June 29, 1964

Many young people who went South were inspired by Allard Lowenstein, a former president of the National Students Association. Lowenstein helped organize students to go to Mississippi in 1963 to work in the civil rights movement.

Civil rights activists in the South often worked under dangerous conditions. In 1964, Rita and Michael Schwerner (right) went to Meridian, Mississippi, to set up a community center for blacks. Bigots threatened to "get the Jew-boy with the beard at Meridian." Andrew Goodman (left) went to Mississippi to help with voter registration. In June 1964, Michael, Andrew, and civil rights worker James Chaney disappeared. They had been kidnapped and murdered by white segregationists.

Rabbi Joachim Prinz (fourth from left), president of the American Jewish Congress, was one of the leaders of the 1963 civil rights march on Washington. Also meeting with President John Kennedy are black leaders Whitney Young, Martin Luther King, Jr., A. Philip Randolph, and Roy Wilkins.

Members of the American Jewish Congress picketing Woolworth's to protest the segregated lunch counters in the store's southern branches.

Martin Luther King, Jr. with ILGWU president David Dubinsky. Under Dubinsky's leadership, the union took a strong stance in support of the civil rights movement.

From left: Roy Wilkins, Sammy Davis, Jr., Kivie Kaplan, and Charles Evers at an NAACP dinner. Kaplan was an officer, fund-raiser, and organizer for the NAACP.

The Unfinished Story

In 1966 blacks took over the leadership of the civil rights movement and began to edge whites out of it. After that, the political relationship between Jews and blacks became increasingly uneasy. Some Jews charged that blacks were anti-Semitic, and some blacks claimed that Jews were racist. Jews were shocked when their stores and buildings were looted and burned during riots in the black ghettos of northern cities. Blacks were disappointed when Jewish parents resisted bussing their children to integrated schools. Some Jews began to wonder whether black political power, educational and employment opportunities could be gained only at the expense of the hard-won Jewish share of the American dream.

The struggle for black equality in America continues. When Jews are called upon to support it, they might remember a teaching of the rabbis: "The day is short and there is much work. . . . You don't have to finish the work, but you are not free to stop doing it."

In March 1985, more than 125 rabbis were arrested at a demonstration to protest the plight of Soviet Jews. Arrested with them was Roy Innis (center), director of the Congress of Racial Equality. "The Jewish people were in the vanguard with us in Selma [Alabama] almost twenty years ago," Innis said. "It was only fair of me to be there at the demonstration and continue my support of Soviet Jewry that started in 1971 with my trip to the Soviet Union."

CLOSE-UPS: *The Struggle for Equality*

The Rosenwalds with their daughter Marion (center) during one of their trips to Tuskegee. The Rosenwalds invited reporters, social workers, and others to be their guests on these trips, to introduce them to life at Tuskegee.

THE ROSENWALD FUND

When Julius Rosenwald was young and newly married, he wanted to make a contribution to a Jewish charity that was more than he could afford. "Don't ever hesitate, Jule, to give money," his wife Augusta said to him. "I will never stand in the way of any gift you want to make."

Rosenwald became president of Sears, Roebuck and Company. He and Augusta followed the advice of their rabbi, Emil G. Hirsch of the Chicago Sinai Congregation, who said, "If you want to prove you have a mission, live it, act it." The Rosenwalds acted to help uneducated blacks in America. They donated millions to improve black education in the South.

The Rosenwalds gave money to support Tuskegee Institute, a black school in Alabama. In 1917, they established the Rosenwald Fund, which by 1932, had set up more than five thousand black elementary schools. At its peak, between 25 and 40 percent of all black children in the rural south were being educated in Rosenwald schools. The Fund also contributed money to black universities and hospitals and provided scholarships for talented blacks.

Rosenwald Fund projects were financed partly by the Fund and partly by local governments and individual whites and blacks in the communities involved. Poor blacks sometimes contributed their share in labor. The Rosenwalds did not want blacks to think of the program as charity but as a way for them to help themselves.

A HOUSEWIFE FIGHTS SEGREGATION

In 1948, Esther Swirk Brown, a young Jewish housewife, saw the two-room shack that was the black public school in South Park, Kansas, and was shocked by its terrible condition. She persuaded the local NAACP lawyer to file a lawsuit to force the local white school to admit black students. She organized a boycott of the black school, set up temporary classes for its students in private homes, and raised money to support the lawsuit and classes. As a result of her activities, her husband Paul was fired from his job, a cross was burned on their lawn, and white neighbors threatened to burn down their house.

After the South Park lawsuit was won, Esther found a black man in Topeka named Oliver Brown whose daughter attended a segregated school. She pushed the local NAACP branch to sue in his name and the case, *Brown* versus *Board of Education*, resulted in the Supreme Court's decision outlawing segregated public schools. "I don't know whether we could have done it without her," said the secretary of Topeka's NAACP.

To fight prejudice on a personal level, Esther directed the Panel of American Women, a national volunteer movement of women of every race and religion who spoke to community groups about their own experiences with prejudice. Esther said she wanted to reach out to parents, "those who are in the best position to reduce prejudice by the example they set their children."

When Esther Brown died in 1970, a local black newspaper said, "If there were more like her in the world, the struggle for justice and equality would have been over long ago."

Esther Brown with Sidney Lawrence (left) of the Jewish Community Relations Bureau and Carl Johnson, president of the Kansas City, Missouri NAACP.

Charles Mantinband

back, I'll give it to you," Mantinband said, "but you can't tell me how to live my personal life." In 1962, the Stephen Wise Free Synagogue in New York gave Mantinband an award for "devotion to individual freedom and social justice, in the spirit of the Hebrew prophets."

From left: Martin Luther King, Jr. with civil rights workers Mickey Shur (now Rabbi Moshe Shur) and Peter Geffen, in the summer of 1965.

A DIXIELAND RABBI

Charles Mantinband was raised in Virginia, where he attended segregated schools. He came North to go to college, and in one of his classes was told to sit next to a black student. When he protested, the professor said, "You had better change your way of thinking." Mantinband did, and as rabbi of congregations in Alabama, Mississippi, and Texas, he became known for his early and courageous support of equal rights for blacks. "I vowed that I would never sit in the presence of bigotry," he said, and not "make my opposition felt."

Mantinband was a member of the Southern Regional Council, a group of white and black community leaders who tried to improve racial conditions in the South through research and action programs. He also served as president of the bi-racial Mississippi Council on Human Relations. He was a frequent speaker at black colleges in the South.

He did this in spite of death threats from the community and pressure from Jews who were afraid they would suffer because of the rabbi's activities. One synagogue board member tried to force the rabbi to stop inviting blacks to his home, saying that the house belonged to the synagogue. "If you want your house

A STUDENT GOES SOUTH

In the summers of 1965 and 1966, nineteen-year-old Peter Geffen went South to work in the civil rights movement. Peter's father, a Conservative rabbi from Atlanta, Georgia, had left the South because he could not live with the racial injustice there. Peter had received a Jewish education and had been president of the national Conservative youth group. The combination of his father's values and his own religious training made him feel that, as a Jew, he had a duty to help blacks get equal rights.

Peter worked for the Southern Community Organization and Political Education project. He toured the South Carolina countryside talking to poor black farmers. He urged them to try to register to vote, taught them what they needed to know to pass the voter registration test, and campaigned for liberal political candidates.

Peter's classmate Andrew Goodman was murdered in Mississippi by racists in 1964. Peter knew that while he was in the South he had reason to be scared. The Ku Klux Klan, an organization of white bigots, was active in South Carolina. Buildings were shot at while Peter was in them, and local churches were bombed.

Peter's experience in South Carolina was not the only example of his commitment to social activism. In June 1967, a few days before the Arab-Israeli war broke out, he flew to Israel to work as a civilian volunteer. After Martin Luther King, Jr. was killed in 1968, Peter marched in the honor guard at his funeral.

Mantinband teaching a class at a black college in the South.

FROM OUR JEWISH HERITAGE: Education

A major goal of the civil rights movement has been equal educational opportunities for blacks. What does our Jewish heritage teach us about the importance of education?

Education at Sinai

When God and Israel entered into the Covenant, the people of Israel agreed to obey God's laws. In order to do this, they first had to learn what God's laws were. God called Moses to Sinai and taught him the commandments. Then Moses gathered the people of Israel together "so that they may hear and learn" the words of the law. (Deuteronomy 31:12) Moses taught the people of Israel what God expected of them, and so was called "Moshe *rabeinu*," or Moses our teacher. One could say that Sinai was a big classroom, the beginning of Jewish education.

Teaching the Generations

What was learned at Sinai must be passed down to each generation. For this purpose, the Jewish family may be seen as a center of learning. Parents are commanded to teach their children about Jewish law and history. (Deuteronomy 11:19) Children are told to "ask your father and he will show you." (Deuteronomy 32:7) They are warned, "forsake not your mother's teachings." (Proverbs 6:20) From the *mezuzah* on the doorpost filled with quotations from the Bible, to the Passover seder that retells the story of the exodus from Egypt, rituals in the Jewish home are a part of a child's education about Judaism.

"Get yourself a teacher," urged the rabbis. Jews are obliged to continue learning throughout their lives. Because studying is

Moses and the Ten Commandments, a detail from the ark at Temple B'rith Kodesh, in Rochester, New York.

A father and son study Talmud together.

a basic part of the Jewish religion, the Jewish people have developed a love of learning and a respect for education, teachers, and scholars. With such an attitude, it is not surprising that Jewish parents emphasize the importance of schoolwork and make every sacrifice to be sure that their children are educated.

Living Judaism

After Moses read the book of the Covenant to the people, they said, "We will do and obey." (Exodus 24:7) The main purpose of study of Torah is to learn the commandments so that they may be fulfilled. It is not just the *study* of Torah that is important, but the *practice* of Torah that is the heart of Jewish life. As the rabbis said, we learn in order to teach, to observe, and to perform. Living Jewishly means putting Torah into action.

The Polonies Talmud Torah of Congregation Shearith Israel, in New York, is the oldest Jewish religious school still operating in this country. It was founded in 1803.

The Jewish Theological Seminary of America, in New York, the center of learning of Conservative Judaism. Other Jewish institutions of higher learning include Yeshiva University in New York (Orthodox); Jewish Institute of Religion-Hebrew Union College, in Cincinnati, Los Angeles, and New York (Reform); and the Reconstructionist Rabbinical College in Philadelphia.

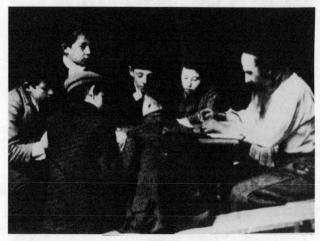

An early twentieth century ḥeder (religious school).

TORAH IN ACTION
Rabbis and Civil Rights

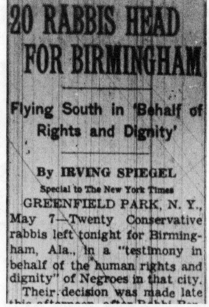

In 1948, Rabbi Jacob Rothschild told his congregants at The Temple in Atlanta, Georgia that he was disturbed by "the growing race hatred that threatens the South." Always outspoken in favor of equality for blacks, Rothschild conducted seminars in the synagogue on civil rights and made speeches urging integration in schools, hotels, and restaurants. He is shown (right) with the mayor of Atlanta, in the ruins of The Temple after it was bombed by racists in 1958.

In May 1963, the Rabbinical Assembly (Conservative) convention voted unanimously to send a delegation to Birmingham, Alabama, to show support for Martin Luther King, Jr. and the civil rights demonstrations he was leading there. The rabbis wanted blacks to know that Jews "were behind them in their struggle, that we had gone from slavery to freedom, and we knew they would."

Rabbi Abraham Joshua Heschel, scholar and professor at the Jewish Theological Seminary, joined the civil rights movement because he believed that "to care for our brother ardently, actively, is a way of worshiping God." He is shown (front row, second from right) marching from Selma to Montgomery in 1965, along with (from his right) Ralph Bunche, Martin Luther King, Jr., and Ralph Abernathy.

16 Rabbis Arrested as Pool Dive-In Sets Off St. Augustine Rights Clash

Policeman dives into pool at the Monson Motor Lodge in St. Augustine, Fla., to arrest the civil rights demonstrators

In response to a request from Martin Luther King, Jr., sixteen Reform rabbis flew to St. Augustine, Florida in June 1964, to demonstrate against segregation. When they tried to integrate a restaurant and swimming pool, the rabbis were arrested. From jail, they issued a statement saying, "We came as Jews who remember the millions of faceless people who stood quietly, watching the smoke rise from Hitler's crematoria. We came because we know that, second only to silence, the greatest danger to man is loss of faith in man's capacity to act."

In July 1964, Rabbi Arthur Lelyveld of Cleveland went to Hattiesburg, Mississippi to work with young civil rights activists. He was returning from voter registration work when he was brutally attacked by two white men who opposed the movement for black equality. "I went to Mississippi," Rabbi Lelyveld told his congregation, "because there are times when conscience demands of one more than words."

In 1961, Rabbi Perry Nussbaum of Jackson, Mississippi organized religious services for civil rights workers of all faiths who had been arrested. "All men are brothers, whatever the color of their skin," he told his congregants. Nussbaum is shown here in his temple study, just after it was bombed (1967). Two months later, his home was bombed and he and his wife narrowly escaped injury.

CLOSE-UPS: *They Came Seeking Freedom*

Sonja Roschko

Jews being herded into the Lodz ghetto.

A TEENAGER IN NAZI GERMANY

Sonja Roschko of Berlin was the leader of her class chorus. One day, the teacher handed her the Horst Wessel song, the official song of the Nazi party, and told her to teach it to the students. Sonja said, "Oh, no, we are not going to sing this." "Why not?" her classmates asked. "Listen to these words," Sonja said, reading them aloud. " 'When Jewish blood spurts from the knife, things will go much better.' " "Why shouldn't we sing the song?" her friends asked again. Amazed at their reaction, Sonja realized that the people she had known for years had become strangers to her. She sat down and refused to conduct the song.

By 1936, persecution of Jews had become so harsh that the Roschkos decided to leave Germany. But it was hard for Jews to get visas to enter other countries. Sonja's parents applied for visas to England, where they had friends. Sonja wanted to go to America, the land of her dreams that she knew from the movies. She went to the American embassy and requested a visa.

In May 1939, her parents' visa came through and they left for England. Sonja stayed behind, still waiting for an American visa. On September 1, 1939, Germany invaded Poland and World War II began. Sonja Roschko was safe. Her visa had arrived just three weeks before and she was on her way to America.

CONCENTRATION CAMP SURVIVORS

In 1942, the Germans expelled the last of the Jews from the Polish town of Ozorkov. Leibel Konstam was among those sent to the ghetto in the nearby city of Lodz. People lived there in terrible conditions, crowded

into unheated apartments, without food or medicine. Two years later, most of the Jews in the Lodz ghetto were sent to the concentration camp at Auschwitz. Later, Leibel was transferred to three other camps.

At the end of the war, Leibel was in Bergen-Belsen, a former camp in Germany that was being used as temporary housing for refugees. There, he met Mindla Lewin. Like Leibel, Mindla had survived Auschwitz and several other death camps. Mindla was also from Ozorkov and had known Leibel before the war. They knew each other's families and had memories to share. In May 1946, Mindla and Leibel were married. Two of their children, Abie and Goldie, were born in Germany.

The Konstams wanted to go to America because as Leibel said, "it was separated from Europe by an ocean." They hated all of Europe, with its memories of family and friends whom the Germans had murdered. They wanted to get as far away as possible from their past.

The Konstams were not able to get visas for America until 1951. Their daughter Hadasa, "our first American," was born ten months after their arrival.

Mindla and Leibel Konstam with their daughter Goldie, soon after their arrival in America (1951).

Perlette Shoueka (right, rear), her children (in front), and relatives at an Egyptian beach.

FLIGHT FROM EGYPT

The Jews of modern Egypt got along well with their Moslem neighbors. They were in business together, they attended each other's weddings. Maurice Shoueka played with the Moslem children on his street. They called him "Mussa," Arabic for "Moses."

But there were some Egyptians who regarded the Jews as foreigners, and hated them because of their religion. In 1945, these fanatics led riots against the Jews. Maurice's mother, Perlette, was sure that Egypt was no longer a safe place for Jews to live. She convinced her husband Yousef to apply for American visas.

After the creation of the State of Israel, there was increasing persecution of Egypt's Jews. Jewish businesses were burned, hundreds of Jews were killed or wounded. Maurice watched in horror from his kitchen window as mobs of Egyptians invaded the Jewish section of Cairo. They took the Torahs from the synagogue behind Maurice's home and burned them. Then they bombed the synagogue.

In the winter of 1948, Maurice was attacked by a group of Moslem children as he stepped off the school bus. "Sahyouni!" they shouted in Arabic. "Zionist!" They threw rocks at his head. His scalp was bloodied and stitches were required to close the wounds. Perlette was more anxious than ever to leave Egypt. It took five years for their visas to arrive. Finally, in 1950, the Shouekas sailed from Alexandria to New York.

Peter Steinreich and Veronica Eckmann just before they left Hungary in 1956.

REVOLUTION IN HUNGARY

Peter Steinreich was born in Hungary in 1942. His parents were killed during World War II. Peter survived because he was sent to the countryside to live with a non-Jewish family that hid him from the Nazis. After the war, he was reunited with his mother's family in Budapest. They were observant Jews. Peter's grandfather, Mihaly Grossman, was cantor of the Dohany Street synagogue, the largest synagogue in Europe.

In 1956, the Hungarian people revolted against the Communists. The Hungarian-Catholic cardinal made a speech on the radio, in which he said, "This is the time for all Christian Hungarians to unite." Where did this leave the Jews? Many of them heard the cardinal's speech and decided to leave their homeland. They had suffered enough because of Hungarian anti-Semitism.

Budapest was in ruins and there was confusion throughout the country. Border guards had been called to fight in the city and had left the borders loosely guarded. Peter went with his aunt, Mancy Eckmann, an Auschwitz survivor, and her husband, Miklos. They snuck across the border carrying the Eckmann's infant daughter Veronica.

Peter and the Eckmanns made their way to an American air base in Germany. From there, they flew to Charleston, South Carolina. They were taken to the army's Camp Kilmer in New Jersey, where along with thousands of other Hungarian refugees, they were allowed to enter America because of a special order issued by President Eisenhower.

LEAVING CASTRO'S CUBA

In 1930, David Perez founded a Jewish day school in Havana, Cuba. The school became known as the Instituto Albert Einstein and for the next thirty-one years, David was its principal. David's wife, Reina Maya, taught at the school, too. The pupils studied general subjects as well as Hebrew, Yiddish, Bible, and religion.

When Fidel Castro entered Havana on December 31, 1959, the Instituto had over four hundred students

Perlette, Manya, Yousef, Farida, and Maurice Shoueka: Cairo, 1950.

David Perez crowning a student Queen Esther at the Instituto's annual Purim celebration: Havana, 1955.

The Copelmans: Rumania, 1960.

and thirty-five teachers. The Jews in Cuba had a rich cultural life and they were allowed to worship freely.

So why did the Perez family leave Havana? First, Cuban officials began demanding changes in the school's courses. The government took over many businesses, and as people began to leave Cuba, the school lost many students. Then all private schools were nationalized, including the Instituto. David was invited to stay on as the Instituto's principal, but he felt he had lost control of his school.

The final blow was Castro's announcement that all children over the age of twelve would have to work in the sugar fields from April through September. This meant they would be separated from their families for six months each year. Reina and David decided to send their sons out of Cuba. In March 1961, Leon who was fourteen, and Alberto who was twelve, were among the Cuban-Jewish children brought to America by HIAS. They lived in a foster home until July, when their parents were able to get American visas and join them.

BRINGING JEWS OUT OF RUMANIA

In 1948, Robert Copelman and his wife Lilian, applied for permission to emigrate from Bucharest, Rumania to the newly created State of Israel. At first, the Rumanian government issued exit permits to Jews who wanted to leave. Rumania was so anti-semitic, Robert said, that "every Jew who left was blessed by the whole country." But later the Rumanians realized that the Jews who were leaving were engineers, lawyers, doctors, intellectuals. They would be a loss to Rumania and would help make Israel strong. Robert was a lawyer, and Lilian was a teacher. Their application for an exit permit was denied.

In the early sixties, an English Jew who traded with the Rumanians made a suggestion to the government: he would arrange for the payment of money to the Rumanians if they would allow Jews to leave the country. The Rumanians needed American dollars, so the agreed, unofficially, to the plan. Thousands of Jews were brought out of Rumania. An American businessman who knew Lilian's family paid $10,000 to a secret bank account in Switzerland. The Copelmans, their daughter Dina, Lilian's brother and his wife were all given exit visas.

The Copelmans took a train from Bucharest to Rome in October 1961. Funds from the Joint Distribution Committee helped support them for ten months in Rome, while HIAS arranged for an American visa. They arrived in New York in 1962 and became American citizens on Robert's brithday— October 25, 1967.

Leon, Reina, David, and Alberto Perez: Havana, 1959.

Yelena, Luba, and Yevgeny Ostashevsky: Leningrad, 1979.

FROM EAST TO WEST

In 1967, after the Israeli victory in the six-day war, there was a growth of pride among Jews in the Soviet Union. On Simḥat Torah of that year, Yelena and Iosif Ostashevsky joined the thousands who gathered at the Leningrad Synagogue. To the Communists, any expression of Jewish feeling was viewed as a form of protest against the Soviet government. Police blocked off the streets near the synagogue and many people were arrested. Among them was Iosif, whose name and photograph were taken. Two of his friends were also arrested and were expelled from school. Fortunately, both Iosif and Yelena had already graduated from the university.

Yelena and Iosif loved their native land, but they longed for the personal freedom they lacked in the Soviet Union. They also were worried about their children's future. Although the Soviet government did not have an official policy of anti-Semitism, passports were stamped *Yivrei* ("Jew"). Especially after 1967, it was hard for a Jew to get into college. The Ostashevskys sometimes thought about leaving the Soviet Union.

Iosif Ostashevsky with Yelena's mother, Zemfira Barshtak, who emigrated to America with her family: Leningrad, 1979.

In 1979, Iosif was offered a promotion. His new job required a security clearance which would allow him to see Soviet state secrets. The problem was that people who knew state secrets were not allowed to leave the Soviet Union, so if he got clearance, he would never be able to emigrate. But if he didn't apply for clearance, it was a sure sign that he was thinking about leaving. Iosif was in a trap.

If the Ostashevskys wanted to emigrate, it had to be now. Iosif refused to apply for clearance and was fired. In 1979, more than fifty thousand Jews were permitted to leave the Soviet Union. The Ostashevskys were among them.

Fatollah, Shirin, Herzel, and Paricher Hakimi: Tehran, 1979.

ESCAPE FROM IRAN

Under the Shah of Iran, Jews were allowed to live peacefully and worship freely. But in 1978, there was increasing opposition to the Shah from strict Moslems led by Ayatollah Khomeini. There were riots, schools were closed, food and heating oil were hard to get. Some Iranians feared that if a revolution came, there would be a loss of freedom. Many people, including Moslems, left Iran.

In the Jewish community, there were frightening rumors. Revolutionaries were warning the Jews, "Just wait until Khomeini comes; we will take care of you Jews." Strange markings were found on the doorways of some Jewish homes. The Jews did not know what these markings meant, but they felt threatened and frightened by them.

Fatollah Hakimi, his wife Paricher, and their children Herzel and Shirin, did not want to take a chance on what life might be like after the revolution. They left Iran just before Khomeini came to power in 1979. Fatollah returned to Tehran to settle his business affairs. When he tried to leave again, he was stopped at the airport. Khomeini's officials gave him no reason for their refusal to allow him to emigrate.

After several months of trying to get permission to leave, Fatollah decided to sneak out of the country. He drove to northwest Iran, walked over the mountains for five hours, and entered Turkey. From there, he rejoined his family. The Hakimis later came to America to be near their married daughter Ruth.

America's Jews today (left to right, top to bottom): A father tells the story of Pesaḥ to his son; a wedding hora; a grandmother watches her grandson read the Purim Megillah; a fund-raising luncheon for Israel Bonds; a grandfather at morning prayers; a demonstration for Soviet Jews; parents blessing their children before Shabbat dinner; an American family at the Knesset in Israel; ultra-Orthodox Jews in Brooklyn; a protest against anti-Israel actions by the United Nations.

INDEX

CREDITS

The following abbreviations are used for photograph sources:

ACTWU   Amalgamated Clothing and Textile Workers Union
AJA   American Jewish Archives
AJC   American Jewish Congress
AJHS   American Jewish Historical Society
Hadassah   Hadassah Photo Archives
HIAS   Hebrew Immigrant Aid Society
ILGWU   International Ladies Garment Workers Union Archives
NAACP   National Association for the Advancement of Colored People
NYHS   New York Historical Society
YIVO   YIVO Institute for Jewish Research

Page 1 left, AJHS; right, Museum of the City of New York; 6 top, AJA; bottom, Ticor-Title Guarantee Company, painting by John Ward Dunsmore; 7 both, NYHS; 8 bottom, Shearith Israel Archives; 9 top, Ticor-Title Guarantee Company, painting by John Ward Dunsmore; 10 top left, Shearith Israel Archives, photo by Helene Schwartz Kenvin; 10 bottom, photo by Helene Schwartz Kenvin; 11 top, NYHS; bottom left and right, AJHS; 12 top left, photo by Fred Andrew Kenvin; top right, photo by Howard Kenvin; bottom, photo by Helene Schwartz Kenvin; 13, by Gustave Doré; 14 bottom left, Mount Sinai Hospital; bottom right, Jewish Child Care Association of New York; 15 top left, Visiting Nurse Service of New York; center left, Hadassah; top right, AJC; center right, United Jewish Appeal; bottom right, photo by Helene Schwartz Kenvin; 17 top, AJA/photo by Jack Warner; 20 bottom left and right, photos by Helene Schwartz Kenvin; 21 top and bottom left, photos by Helene Schwartz Kenvin, 21 top right, AJHS; 22 all, AJHS; 23 bottom, Oglethorpe University; 27 top, both, Marion A. (Mrs. B.H.) Levy; bottom, information courtesy of Malcom Stern, *First American Jewish Families*, calligraphy by Kathleen Borowick; 28, AJA/Congregation Mickve Israel (Savannah) and Rabbi Saul Rubin; 29 top, AJA; 30, Ticor-Title Guarantee Company, painting by John Ward Dunsmore; 31 bottom, Mikveh Israel (Philadelphia) Archives; 33 bottom left, AJA; bottom center, AJHS; top left, AJA; top and bottom right, AJHS; 34, painting by Gustave Doré; 35, AJHS; 36, photo by Isaac Berez; 39, NYHS; 40 top, Mikveh Israel (Philadelphia) Archives; 44 top and bottom, AJHS; 46, Helene and Howard Kenvin; 50 top and right, AJHS; 51, AJHS; 52 right, Shearith Israel Archives, photo by Helene Schwartz Kenvin; bottom, lithograph by E.P. and L. Restein; 54 top, AJHS; 55 left, AJHS; right, AJA; 56 left, AJHS; right, AJA; 57 all, AJHS; 58 top, both, AJHS; bottom right, Philip Nathans Steel, Jr.; 59 all, AJHS; 63 top, Marion A. (Mrs. B.H.) Levy; bottom, Abram Minis, Jr.; 64 top and center, AJA; 66 top, Meyer Kairey/Sephardic Archives; center, Joe E. Ash/Sephardic Archives; bottom, Meyer Safdieh/Sephardic Archives; 67 top left, AJHS; top right, Helene Schwartz Kenvin; center middle, Jewish War Veterans; center right, U.S. Department of the Navy; bottom right, Howard S. Levi; 68 top left, right, bottom left, AJA; 69 all, AJA; 70 top left, *Jews in Early Mississippi*, by Leo and Evelyn Turitz, courtesy of the authors/Jane L. Sizeler; top center, *Jews in Early Mississippi*, courtesy of the authors/Frank Friedler; bottom left, *Jews in Early Mississippi*, courtesy of the authors/McComb Enterprise Journal; 70 top and bottom right, AJA; 71 all, AJA; 75 left and center, AJHS; right, AJA; 76 left, AJHS; 77 bottom, AJHS; 78 top, *Frank Leslie's Popular Monthly*, August 1877; bottom, both, AJHS; 79, AJA; 80 top, *Iphigene: Memoirs of Iphigene Ochs Sulzberger* by Sulzberger and Dryfoos; right, AJHS; 81 left, U.S. Army Signal Corps.; 82, Bloch Publishing Co.; 83 left, AJC; 84 bottom left, AJA; 85 top and bottom, AJHS; 86 top, AJA; bottom AJHS; 87 top, AJHS; 88 left, Flora S. and Roger W. Straus; center, AJA; right, AJHS; 89 top, AJA; 90 both, AJHS; 91 top left, AJA; others, AJHS; 92 top right, AJA; others, AJHS; 93 top, *History of Boston*, by J.S. Homans (1856); center and bottom, *The Peres Family*, by Sam Shankman (1938); 94 both, AJA; 95 top, both, Minnesota Historical Society; bottom, AJA; 96 top left, AJA; top right, sketch drawn at the scene by Frederick Remington, from *On the Bloody Trail of Geronimo*, by John Bigelow, Jr., Westernlore Press; bottom left and right, Historical Association of Southern Florida; 99, YIVO; 100 top, YIVO; 101 both, YIVO; 102 top, Morris Wiesenthal; 103 top, YIVO; left, engraving by C.J. Staniland (1892); 104 top left, Michael Brenner; top right and center, Marc Angel; bottom left, Helene Schwartz Kenvin; bottom right, Shraga Gottesfeld; 106 top, Helene Schwartz Kenvin; bottom Ethel and Melvin Schwartz; right, Arye Barkai; 107 left, Norma Solomon and Carol Goldberger; others, Helene Schwartz Kenvin; 108 top, Sam Angel; bottom, Belle Goodman Kenvin; 109 left, Rachel Levy Angel; top and bottom right, Helene Schwartz Kenvin; bottom left, Morris Wiesenthal; 110 top left, Haim Golan; bottom, photo by Helene Schwartz Kenvin; top right, Daniel Kenvin; 111, by Gustave Doré; 112 top, Helene and Howard Kenvin; others, photos by Helene Schwartz Kenvin; 113 top left, Neil and Goldie Ellman; center, Howard Kenvin; others, photos by Helene Schwartz Kenvin; 114 right, ACTWU; left, AJA; 115 top left and top left center, Helene Schwartz Kenvin; top right, top right center, Howard Kenvin; center left, Helene Schwartz Kenvin, center right, ILGWU; bottom left, Helene Schwartz Kenvin; bottom right, ACTWU; 116 top left, Helene Schwartz Kenvin; others, ACTWU; 117 top, AJHS; center, YIVO; bottom, photo by Helene Schwartz Kenvin; 118 top, photo by Helene Schwartz Kenvin; bottom, *La America: The Sephardic Experience in the United States*, by Marc Angel, courtesy of the author; 119 top, Richard Levie; bottom, AJHS; 120 both, Alliance Colony Foundation; 121 top and bottom left, YIVO; right, AJHS; 122 top and center, AJA; 123 all, National Council of Jewish Women, New York Section; 124 top and bottom left, photos by Helene Schwartz Kenvin; top and bottom right, Visiting Nurse Association of New York; 126 top, photo by Helene Schwartz Kenvin; bottom, Helene Schwartz Kenvin; 127 top left and center, Alliance Colony Foundation; top right, Frank Hyams; bottom, photo by Helene Schwartz Kenvin; 128, ACTWU; 129 top left, ACTWU; 130 top left, Library of Congress, Bain Collection; top right, Ethel Schwartz; center, Helene Schwartz Kenvin; 131 top, ACTWU; bottom, *Jewish Daily Forward*; 132 bottom, Ethel Schwartz; 133, *Jewish Daily Forward*; 134, Joseph Sultan/Sephardic Archives; 136 top right, Library of Congress, Bain Collection; left, Melvin Schwartz; bottom, photo by Helene Schwartz Kenvin; 137 top, David Hidary/Sephardic Archives; bottom, David Schwartz/Sephardic Archives; 138 top and bottom left, Marsha Saron Dennis; top right, Alliance Colony Foundation and Mollie Greenblatt Kravitz; bottom right, photo by Jay H. Greenblatt; 139 top left and center, bottom left, Melvin C. Schwartz; top right, Marc Angel; bottom right, *La America*, by Marc Angel, courtesy of the author; 140 top left and right, Mary Braca Sultan; bottom, Eileen and Harriet Levine Katasky, Morton Levine; 141 all, Richard Levie; 142 top left, Gary Mokotoff; bottom left, photo by Helene Schwartz Kenvin; top and bottom right, Ethel Schwartz; 143 top and center, Dorothy Dellar Kohanski; 144 top and center left, bottom, ACTWU; top right, drawing by Jacob Epstein; center, Helene Schwartz Kenvin; center right, Ethel Schwartz; 145 bottom, ILGWU; 146 top, ACTWU; others, ILGWU; 147 both, ILGWU; 148 all, ILGWU; 149 top and bottom right, ACTWU; left, AJC; 150 all, ILGWU; 151 all, ACTWU; 152 both, AC-TWU; 153 top right, center, bottom right, ACTWU; top and bottom left, ILGWU; 154 top, ILGWU; 155 top and center, AFLCIO; bottom, ILGWU; 156 top and bottom, ILGWU; 157 right, ILGWU; 158 top and bottom right, ACTWU; 159, by Gustave Doré; 160 bottom, ACTWU; 161 top left, ACTWU; top right, center, bottom left, ILGWU; 162, photo by Helene Schwartz Kenvin; 164 bottom, Jewish War Veterans; 165 top left and right, AJC; bottom, ILGWU; 166 left, AJC; others, ILGWU; 167 left, *The New York Times*; right, AJC; 168 top, Jewish Theological Seminary; 169 top, HIAS and Flora Rothenberg; bottom left, Mollie and Daniel Harris; bottom right, AJC; 170 all, American Joint Distribution Committee; 171 left, AJA; others, Ira Hirschmann; 172 top, Ruth Gruber; bottom, Ruth Gruber and Jack Cohen; 173, Museum of the Diaspora, Tel Aviv; 174, by Paul Davis for the Coalition to Free Soviet Jews; 175 top, AJC; bottom left, B'nai Brith Anti-Defamation League; bottom right, photo by Helene Schwartz Kenvin; 176 top, Official Photo, The White House; bottom, photo by Helene Schwartz Kenvin; 178, AJC; 179 bottom, Hadassah; 180 center right, Abraham J. Klausner; left, both, Hadassah/Official U.N. photos; 181 top, Hadassah; 182 top left and bottom right, Hadassah; top right, photo by Helene Schwartz Kenvin; center, Ethel and Melvin Schwartz; bottom left, Helene Schwartz Kenvin; 183 left, both, AJC; right, Hadassah; 184 top, Hadassah; bottom, AJA; right, UPI/Bettman; 185 left, Hadassah/Official U.N. photo; right, Eli and Shirley Math Stolpner; 186, Bloch Publishing Co.; 187, photo by Helene Schwartz Kenvin; 188 top, AJC; bottom left, Hadassah; bottom right, AJA; 189 top left, AJA; top and bottom right, Hadassah; 190 all, NAACP; 191 center, NAACP; bottom, AJC; 192 top and center, NAACP; bottom, U.S. Department of the Interior; 193 left, NAACP; right, AJC; 194 top right, Dorothy Lowenstein DiCintio; bottom, AJC; 195 top, AJC; bottom left, ILGWU; bottom right, NAACP; 196, photo by Helene Schwartz Kenvin; 197 top, William Rosenwald and Marion Rosenwald Ascoli; bottom, Susan Brown Tucker; 198 top and bottom left; Carol Matinband Ginsberg; right, Peter Geffen; 200 top left, right, photos by Helene Schwartz Kenvin; center left, Shearith Israel Archives; 201 top right, *The New York Times*; 202 top, *The New York Times*/AP-Wide World; bottom left, AP-Wide World; bottom right, Perry Nussbaum; 203 top left, Sonja Roschko Brodheim; bottom, Goldie Konstam Ellman; 204 top and bottom left, Maurice Shoueka; right, Peter Steinreich and Veronica Eckmann Reich; 205 top and bottom left, David and Reina Perez; right, Robert and Lilian Copelman; 206 top and bottom left, Helen and Iosif Ostashevsky; right, Fatollah Hakimi; 207 top right, photo by Melvin Schwartz; second row, center, Israel Bonds; bottom left, Ethel and Melvin Schwartz; others, photos by Helene Schwartz Kenvin.